Fun-schooling

CURRICULUM

HOMESCHOOLING WITH

MINECRAFT

The Beginners Journal

ANIMAL & FARM THEME

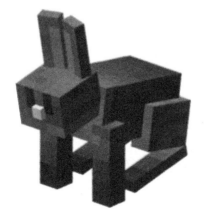

FUNSCHOOLINGBOOKS.COM

THIS CURRICULUM COVERS:

- Reading

- Handwriting

- Logic

- Spelling

- Classical Literature

- Classical Music

- Mathematics

- Addition, Subtraction and Multiplication Practice

- Animals and Habitats

- Geography

- Computer Skills

- Building & Design

- Art, Drawing and Design

- Creative Comics

- Research & Library Skills

- Unit Studies (based on the student's favorite topics)

- Poetry

- Brain Games from Dyslexia Games Series A & B

HOMESCHOOLING WITH MINECRAFT

NAME:

_____

Name of My Minecraft World:

_____

My Age: _____ Date: _____

Contact: _____

By: Sarah Janisse Brown, Isaac Brown
& Tolik Trishkin

We use the Dyslexie Font by Christian Boer

Minecraft Farming Poems By The Frank Family
Farming Prompts By Grant & Carrie Moyers

The Thinking Tree Publishing Company, LLC

INSTRUCTIONS

CHOOSE YOUR TOPICS!

LIST & DRAW EIGHT THINGS that you want to learn about:

1._____
2._____
3._____
4._____
5._____
6._____
7._____
8._____

Complete 3 to 5 pages each day.

ACTION STEPS:

Go to the library or bookstore. Bring home a stack of at least EIGHT interesting books about these topics. Choose some that have diagrams, instructions and illustrations. Choose some books about science, history and social studies related to the topics you want to study.

RECOMMENDED EDUCATIONAL RESOURCES:

- A Computer and Your Own Minecraft World

- Audio Books like Heroes Now & Then• by YWAM

- Story of the World for the Classical Child•

- Classical Music to help you relax while you work

- Tutorials, Educational Movies & Documentaries

- A Math Curriculum like Life of Fred• or Math-U-See•

- DyslexiaGames.com Series A for struggling readers

- Many parents use EPIC's online children's library: www.getepic.com

SCHOOL SUPPLIES NEEDED:

Pencils, Colored Pencils, Gel Pens, Origami Paper, a Ruler

PARENT & CHILD ACTIVITIES:

Turn to the last page to start interesting discussions with your child.

Talk about farming in the real world vs. Minecraft.

Draw a farm together on the last page.

GO TO THE LIBRARY AND CHOOSE EIGHT BOOKS TO USE AS SCHOOL BOOKS!

1. Write down the titles on each cover below.

2. Keep your stack of books in a safe place so you can read a few pages from your books daily.

MONTH:

January

February

March

April

May

June

July

August

September

October

November

December

Pick an animal to learn about today, draw it:

_____

COLOR ME!

How are you FEELING TODAY?

DAY:_____

_____

YEAR:_____

YOU HAVE SEEN THIS ANIMAL ON MINECRAFT.
NOW DESIGN YOUR OWN ANIMAL.

CREATE YOUR OWN CRAFTING RECIPE

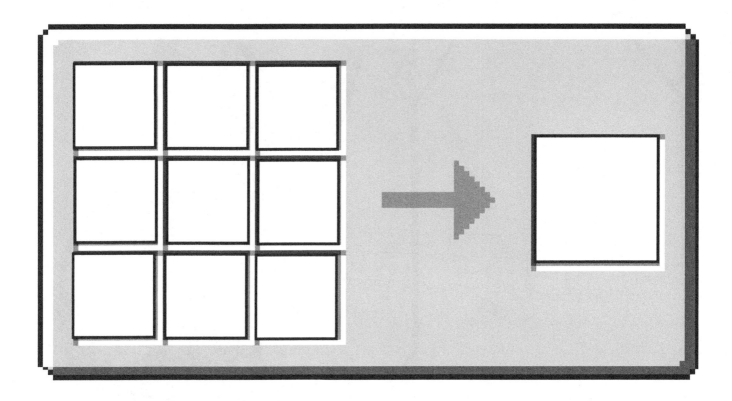

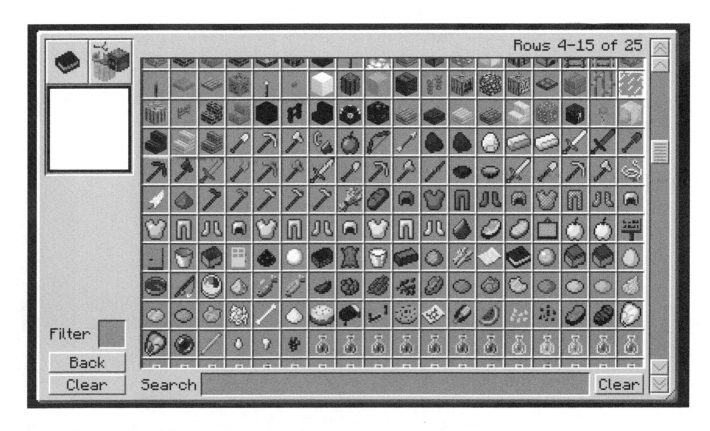

BRAIN GAMES

DRAW ANYTHING

WHat CaN YOU BuiLD?

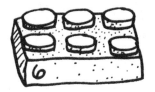 **X6**

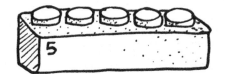 **X6**

 **X6**

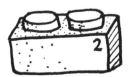 **X6**

 X6

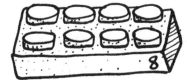 **X6**

Use six of each kind of block.

What did you build?

_____

FiNiSH the PictURe

READING TIME

Write and draw about
what you are learning.

BACKYARD SCIENCE
NATURE WALK & NATURE STUDY

Draw or write about the things you see outside today.

Talk to someone about the difference between real animals and Minecraft animals.

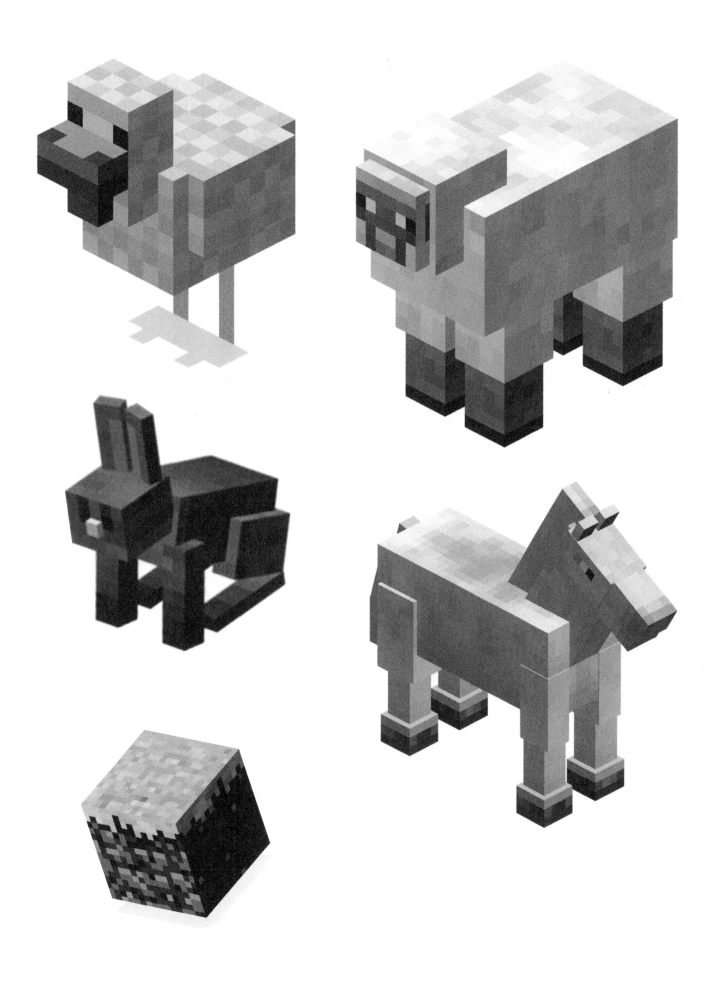

Blocks

MATH PRACTICE

Check Your Work
with a Calculator

42 + 40	10 + 17
12 + 14	13 + 75
23 + 23	20 + 67
46 + 12	30 + 69
230 + 29	134 + 125

CIRCLE THE ITEMS

That Match Each
Answer

289 + 10	310 + 14
245 + 30	201 + 97
100 + 213	324 + 11
200 + 95	234 + 113
22 + 2234	234 + 2023

SPELLING TIME

WORD HUNT

Choose A Letter

_____

Find 10 words that include this letter.

1._____

2._____

3._____

4._____

5._____

6._____

7._____

8._____

9._____

10._____

ANIMALS OF THE WORLD

What animal are you learning about?

_____

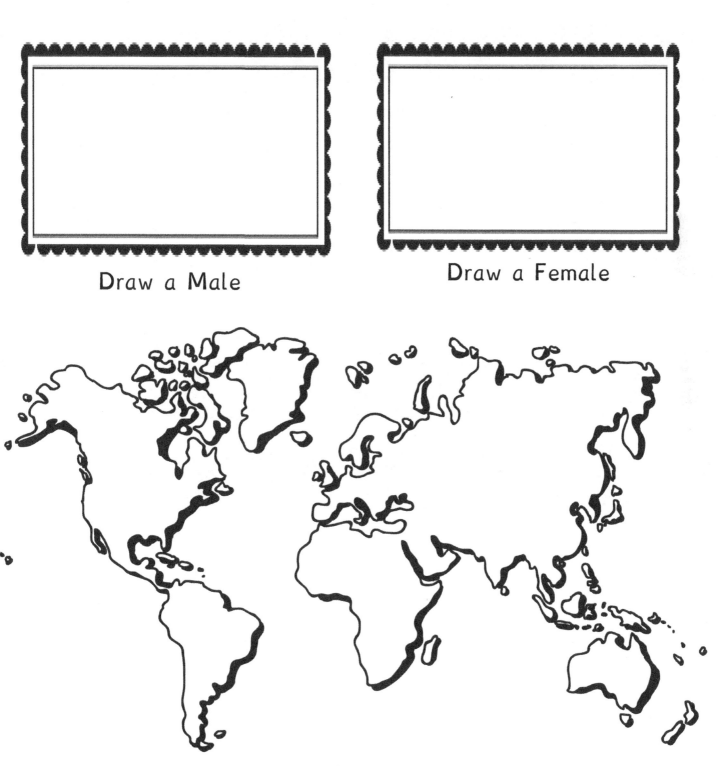

Draw a Male

Draw a Female

Color the parts of the world where this animal lives.

MOVIE TIME

Watch an Educational Film, Tutorial or Documentary.

TITLE:_____

RATING:

Draw Your Favorite Scene:

Write a Review:

_____

_____

_____

_____

_____

MATH TIME

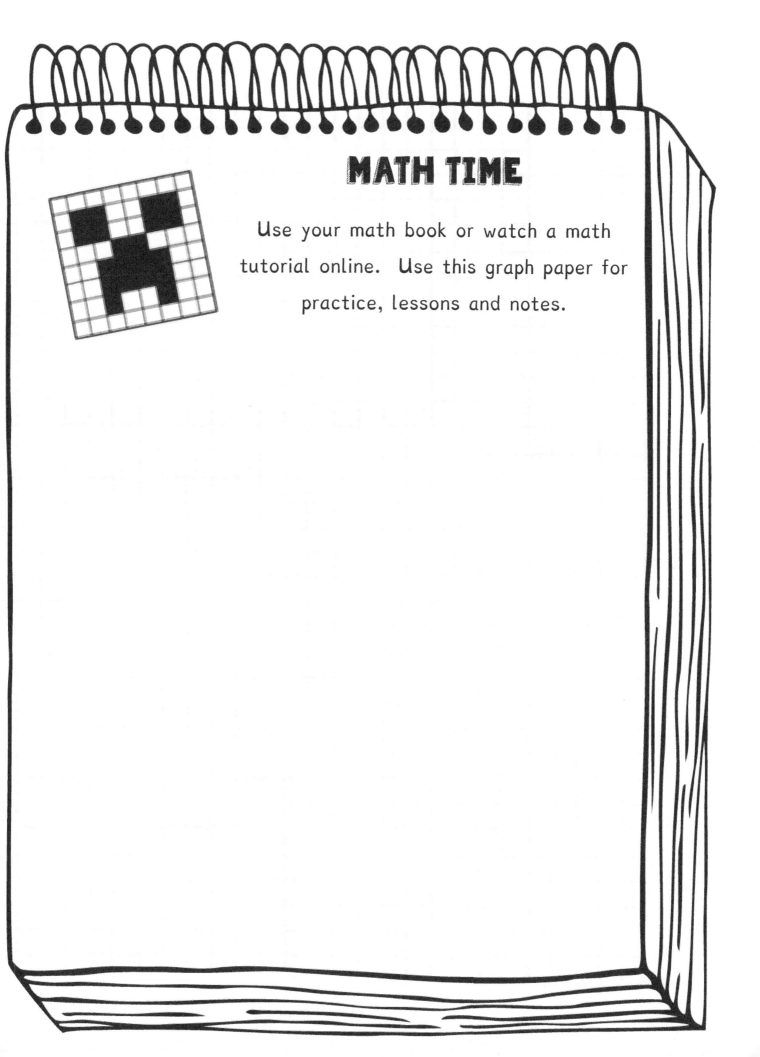

Use your math book or watch a math tutorial online. Use this graph paper for practice, lessons and notes.

MONTH:

January

February

March

April

May

June

July

August

September

October

November

December

POETRY CORNER
Minecraft Haiku

Hunger Bars are low
I will farm the land for food
I am now so full

COLOR ME!

How are you
FEELING TODAY?

DAY: _____

_____

YEAR: _____

BACKYARD SCIENCE
NATURE WALK & NATURE STUDY

Draw or write about the things you see outside today.

READING TIME

Write and draw about what you are learning.

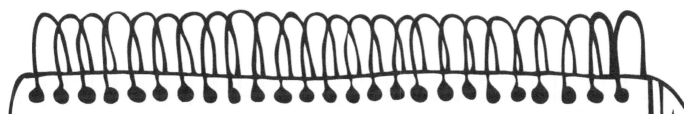

MINECRAFT FARMING

CHALLENGE
DRAW, DESIGN & BUILD

Draw/Design a farmhouse.

Build it in your Minecraft World.

CREATE YOUR OWN CRAFTING RECIPE

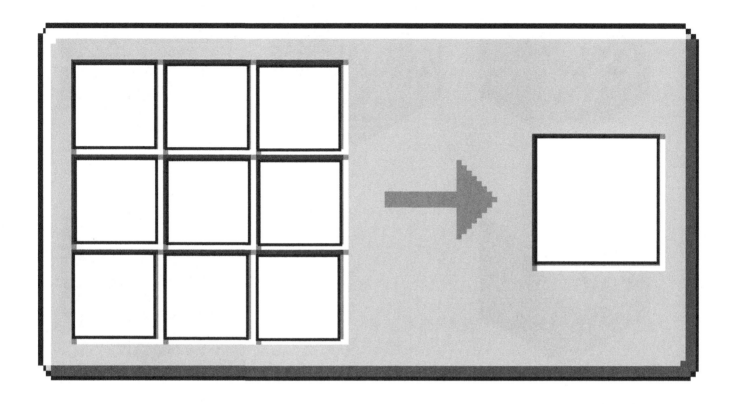

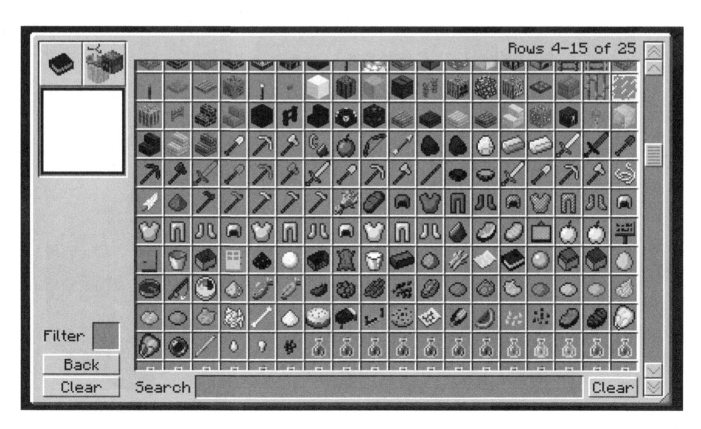

MATH TIME

Use your math book or watch a math tutorial online. Use this graph paper for practice, lessons and notes.

BONUS: Minecraft Math:

How many corners can you count on the

blocks on the opposite page? _____

CAN YOU MAKE IT?

Get a piece of origami paper and follow the instructions.

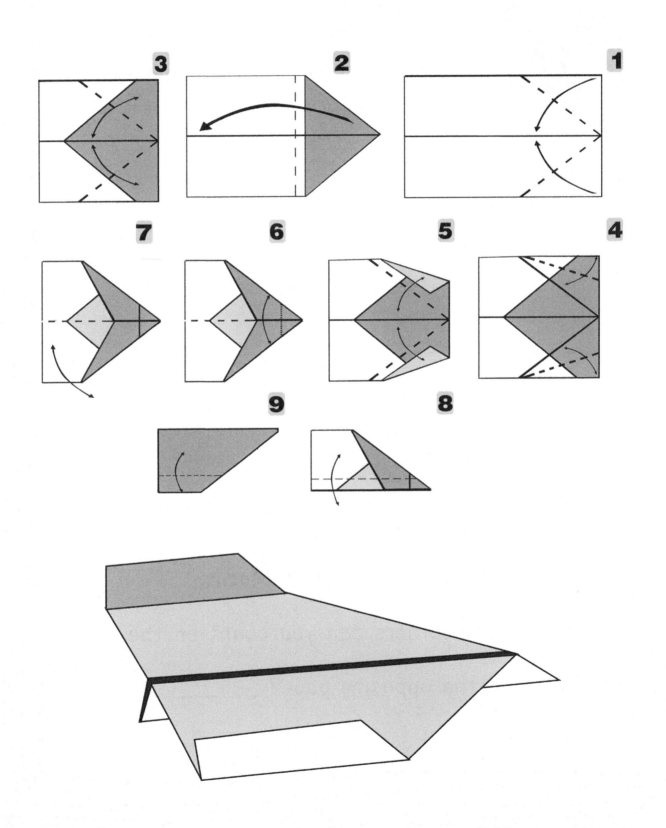

DIGITAL LETTERS

Create your own digital letters and numbers.

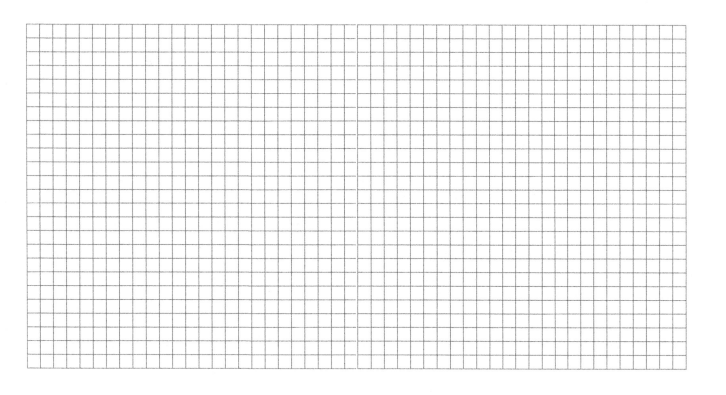

CREATE YOUR OWN CRAFTING RECIPE

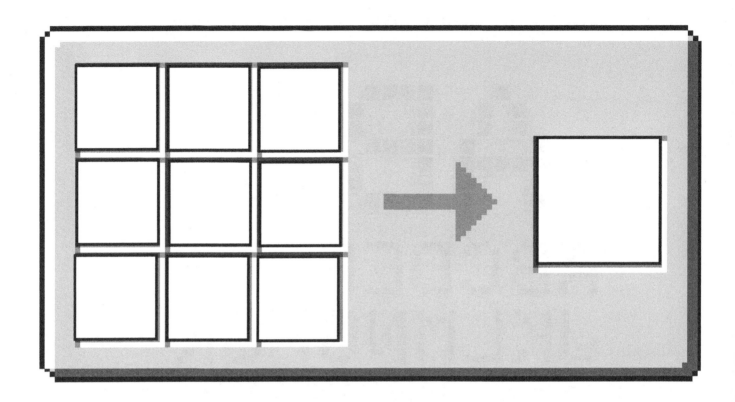

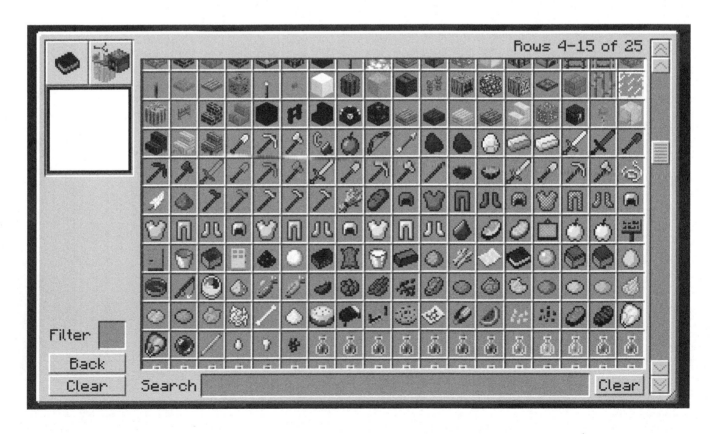

BRAIN GAMES

DRAW ANYTHING

MONTH:

January

February

March

April

May

June

July

August

September

October

November

December

Pick an animal to learn about today, draw it:

_____

How are you FEELING TODAY?

COLOR ME!

DAY:_____

_____

YEAR:_____

LISTENING TIME
CLASSICAL MUSIC, HISTORY & LITERATURE

Listen to Story of the World, an audio book

or classical music. Draw and doodle below.

I am listening to: _____

READING TIME

Write and draw about what you are learning.

BACKYARD SCIENCE
NATURE WALK & NATURE STUDY

Draw or write about the things you see outside today.

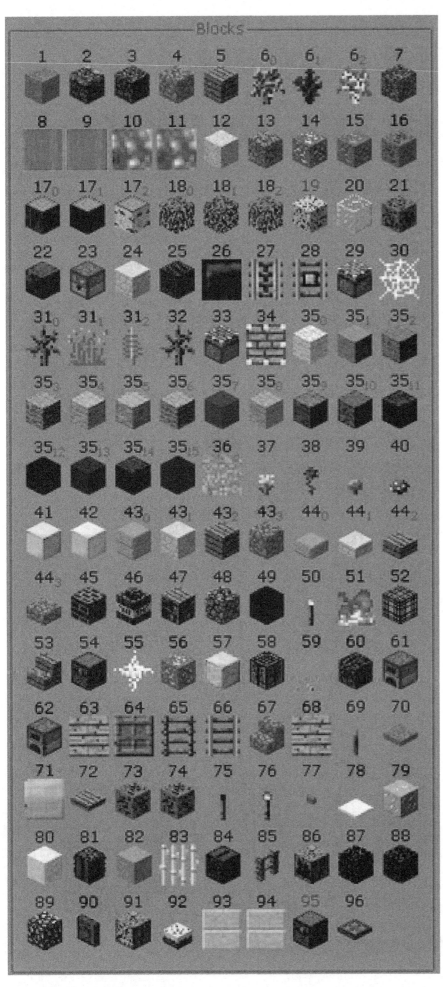

MATH PRACTICE

Check Your Work
with a Calculator

42 + 30	10 + 57
12 + 38	10 + 75
40 + 23	20 + 31
40 + 4	30 + 5
88 + 10	70 + 6

CIRCLE THE ITEMS

That Match Each
Answer

289 + 19	310 + 44
245 + 20	201 + 88
100 + 250	324 + 40
200 + 85	234 + 100
22 + 333	234 + 23

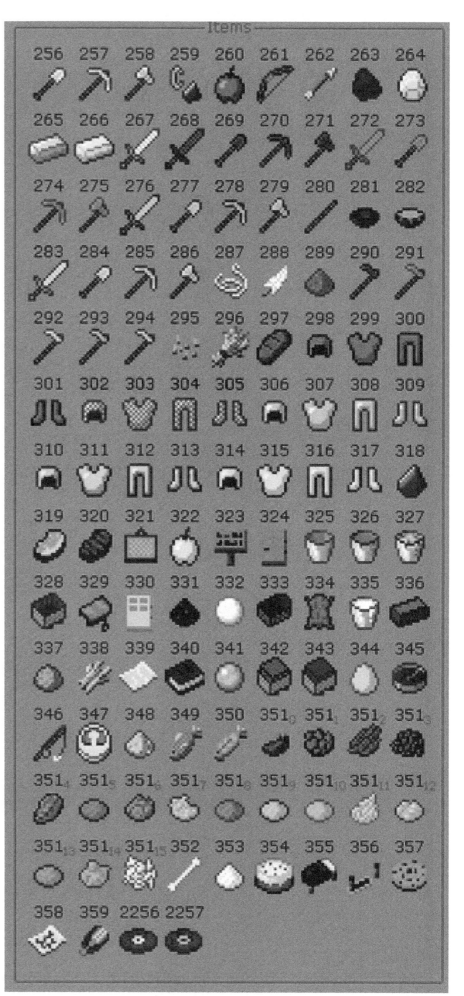

41

WHat Can YOU BuiLd?

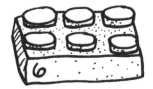 X8

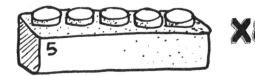 X8

 X8

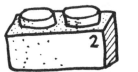 X8

 X8

 X8

Use eight of each kind of block.

What did you build?

_____

FiNiSH tHe PictURe

AN ANIMAL'S LIFE

TYPE OF ANIMAL:_____

BABY

HABITAT

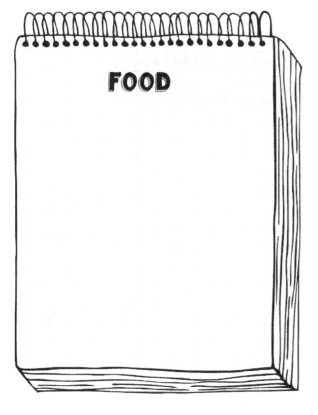

FOOD

ENEMIES

MOVIE TIME

Watch an Educational Film, Tutorial or Documentary.

TITLE:_____

RATING:

Draw Your Favorite Scene:

Write a Review:

_____

_____

_____

_____

_____

MATH TIME

Use your math book or watch a math tutorial online. Use this graph paper for practice, lessons and notes.

YOU HAVE SEEN THIS ANIMAL ON MINECRAFT. NOW DESIGN YOUR OWN ANIMAL.

BRAIN GAMES

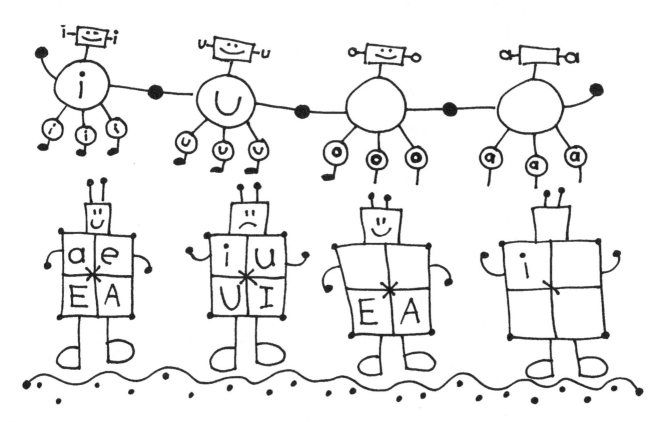

DRAW ANYTHING

MONTH:

January

February

March

April

May

June

July

August

September

October

November

December

POETRY CORNER
Don't Starve

Clear off the land
Plow the field by hand

Planted lots of seeds
Potatoes, Carrots and Beets, no weeds

Water the row
Watch them grow

Cook it all for sup
Keep your hunger bars up

COLOR ME!

How are you FEELING TODAY?

DAY:_____

_____

YEAR:_____

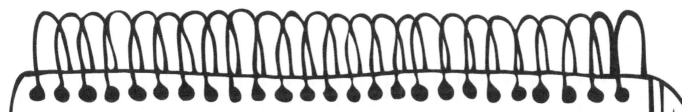

MINECRAFT FARMING

CHALLENGE
DRAW, DESIGN & BUILD

Draw a barn and build it in Minecraft.

Add animals to your barn.

CREATE YOUR OWN CRAFTING RECIPE

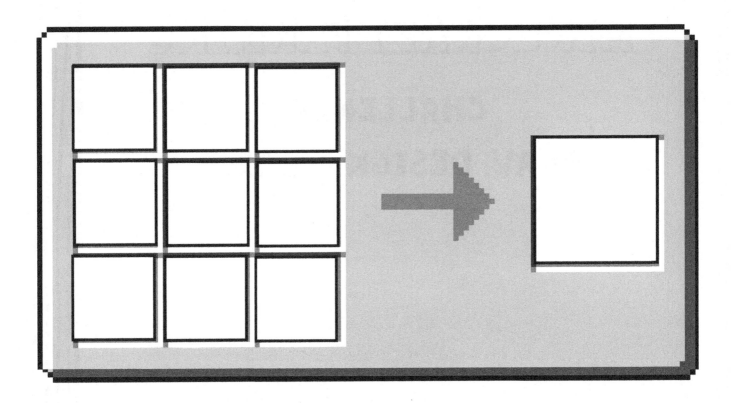

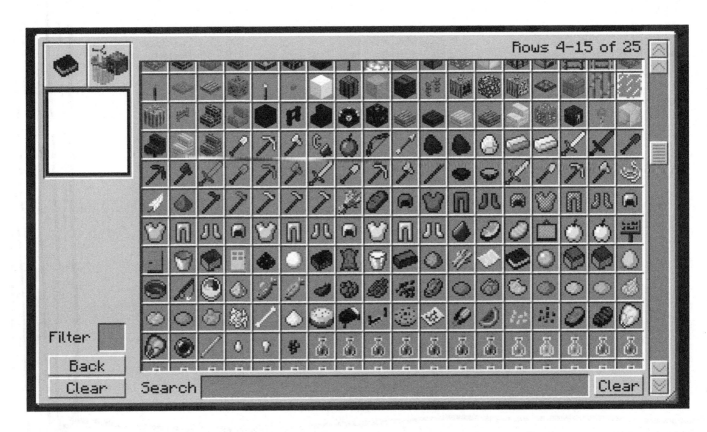

Filter

Back

Clear

Search

Clear

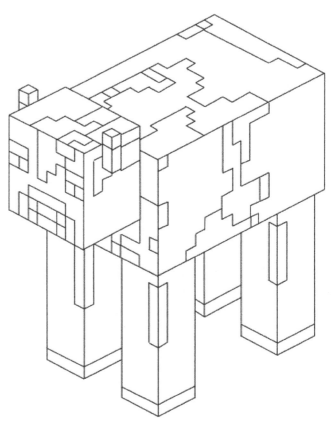

READING TIME

Write and draw about what you are learning.

BACKYARD SCIENCE
NATURE WALK & NATURE STUDY

Draw or write about the things you see outside today.

COMIC STRIP - WHAT HAPPENS NEXT ?

Night is coming and monsters will soon be upon you!

You have no supplies. What will you do?

ART & LOGIC

Draw the Missing Parts

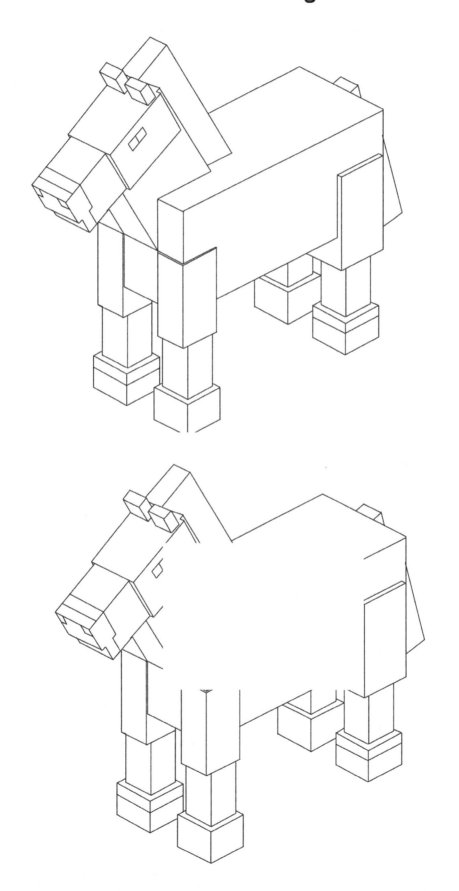

MINECRAFT

Draw and Label Four Elements

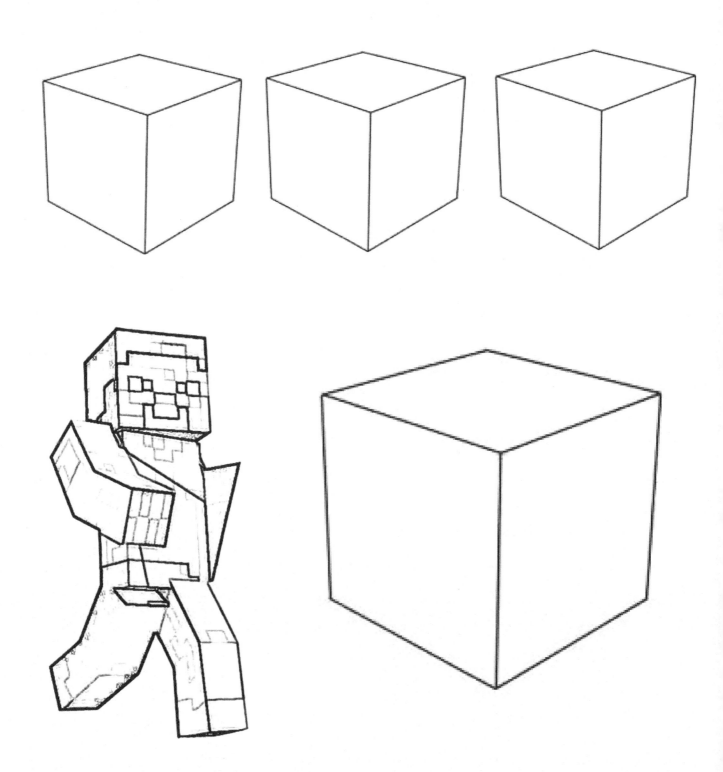

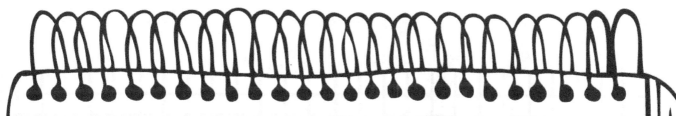

MINECRAFT FARMING

CHALLENGE
DRAW, DESIGN & BUILD

1. A Trap

2. A Fort

3. A Tunnel

MONTH:

January

February

March

April

May

June

July

August

September

October

November

December

Pick an animal to learn about today, draw it:

_____

COLOR ME!

How are you FEELING TODAY?

DAY:_____

_____

YEAR:_____

ART & LOGIC

Draw the Missing Parts

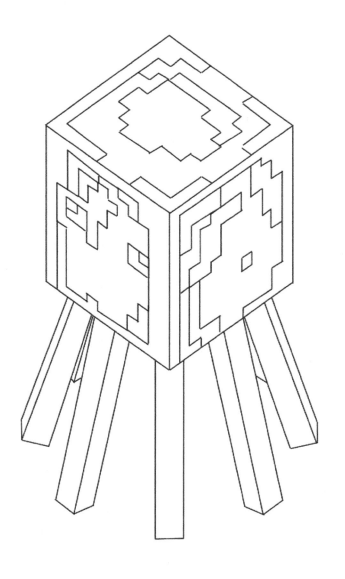

CREATE YOUR OWN CRAFTING RECIPE

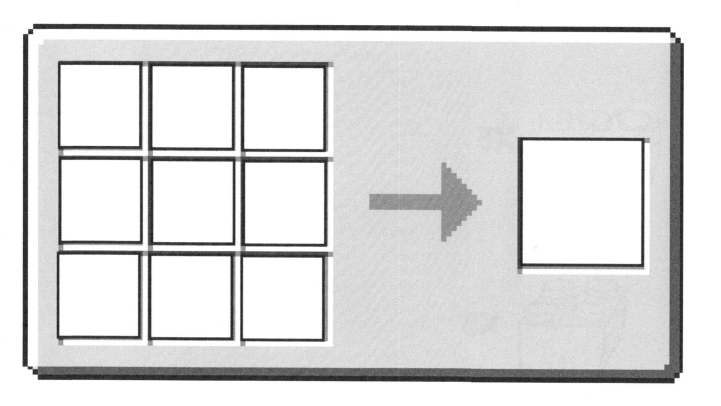

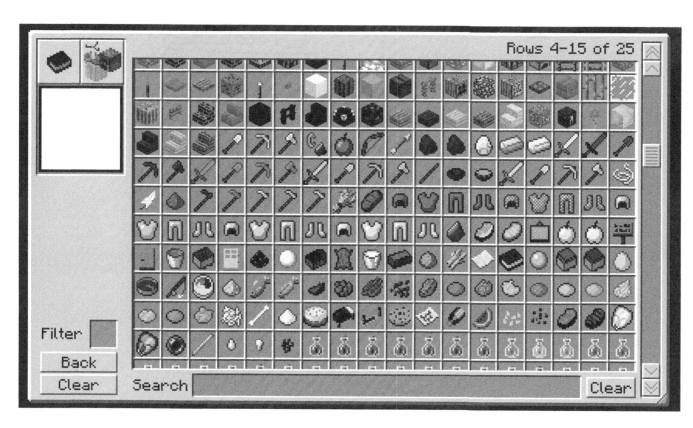

WHat CaN YOU BuiLd?

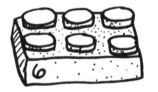 X5

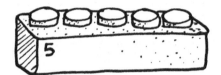 X5

 X5

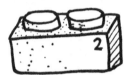 X5

 X5

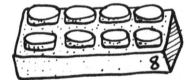 X5

Use five of each kind of block.

What did you build?

_____

FiNiSH the PictuRE

READING TIME

Write and draw about what you are learning.

BACKYARD SCIENCE
NATURE WALK & NATURE STUDY

Draw or write about the things you see outside today.

SPELLING TIME

WORD HUNT

Choose A Letter

Find 10 words that include this letter.

1._____

2._____

3._____

4._____

5._____

6._____

7._____

8._____

9._____

10._____

ANIMALS OF THE WORLD

What animal are you learning about?

_____

Draw a Male

Draw a Female

Color the parts of the world where this animal lives.

MOVIE TIME

Watch an Educational Film, Tutorial or Documentary.

TITLE:_____

Draw Your Favorite Scene:

RATING:

Write a Review:

_____

_____

_____

_____

_____

MATH TIME

Use your math book or watch a math
tutorial online. Use this graph paper for
practice, lessons and notes.

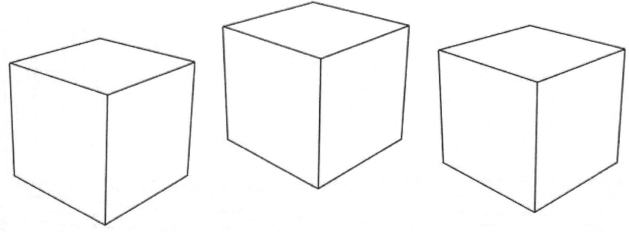

MATH PRACTICE

Check Your Work with a Calculator

42 − 10	10 + 8
100 − 38	12 + 75
40 − 23	70 + 21
40 − 10	30 + 11
88 − 20	70 + 12

CIRCLE THE ITEMS

That Match Each
Answer

289 − 10	210 + 54
345 + 10	301 − 88
559 − 250	304 + 11
200 + 85	457 − 100
700 − 360	234 + 93

AN ANIMAL'S LIFE

TYPE OF ANIMAL:_____

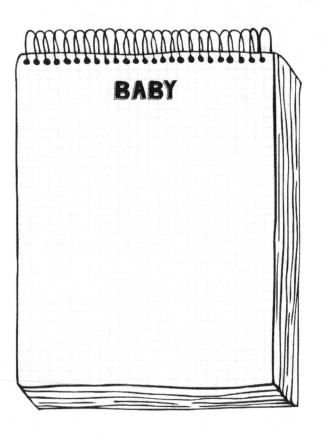

BABY

HABITAT

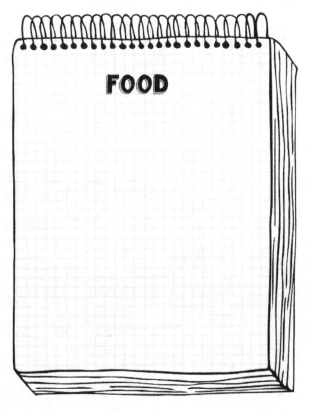

FOOD

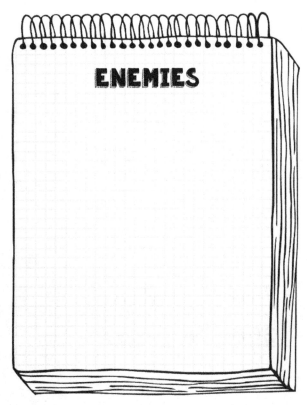

ENEMIES

BRAIN GAMES

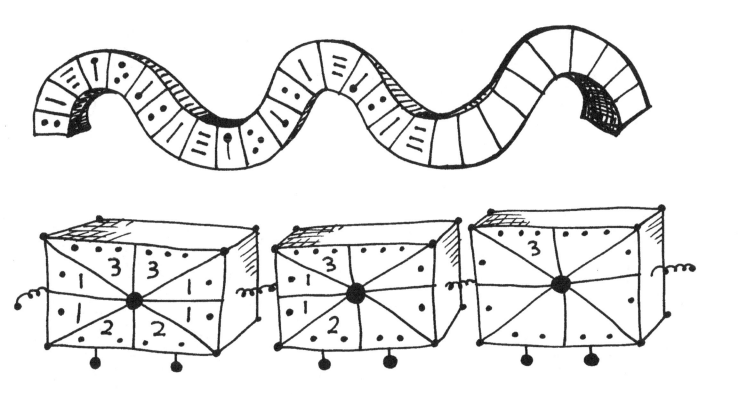

DRAW ANYTHING

BRAIN GAMES

DRAW ANYTHING

Talk to someone about the difference between real cows and Minecraft cows.

MONTH:

January

February

March

April

May

June

July

August

September

October

November

December

Pick an animal to learn about today, draw it:

_____

COLOR ME!

How are you
FEELING TODAY?

DAY:_____

_____

YEAR:_____

MINECRAFT FARMING

CHALLENGE
DRAW, DESIGN & BUILD

Design a chicken coop. Build it in Minecraft.
Add chickens to your coop.

READING TIME

Write and draw about what you are learning.

COPYWORK

Copy a sentence from one of your library books.

TITLE: _____Page#_____

DRAWING TIME

Copy an illustration from one of your books.

COMIC BOOK FONT WRITING PRACTICE

Try different comic book writing styles!

DYSLEXIE FONT BY CHRISTIAN BOER:

ABCDEFGHIJKLMNOPQRSTUVWXYZ

abcdefghijklmnopqrstuvwxyz

Create Your Own Font Here:

MONTH:

January

February

March

April

May

June

July

August

September

October

November

December

POETRY CORNER
Wheat is Yellow

Potatoes are brown
Wheat is yellow
Hauling water buckets from town
Because you're a busy fellow

COLOR ME!

How are you
FEELING TODAY?

DAY:_____

_____

YEAR:_____

LISTENING TIME
CLASSICAL MUSIC, HISTORY & LITERATURE

Listen to Story of the World, an audio book

or classical music. Draw and doodle below.

I am listening to: _____

READING TIME

Write and draw about what you are learning.

BACKYARD SCIENCE
NATURE WALK & NATURE STUDY

Draw or write about the things you see outside today.

CREATE YOUR OWN CRAFTING RECIPE

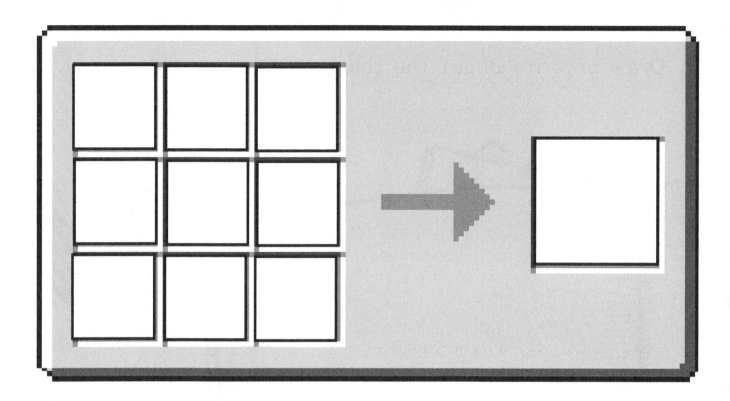

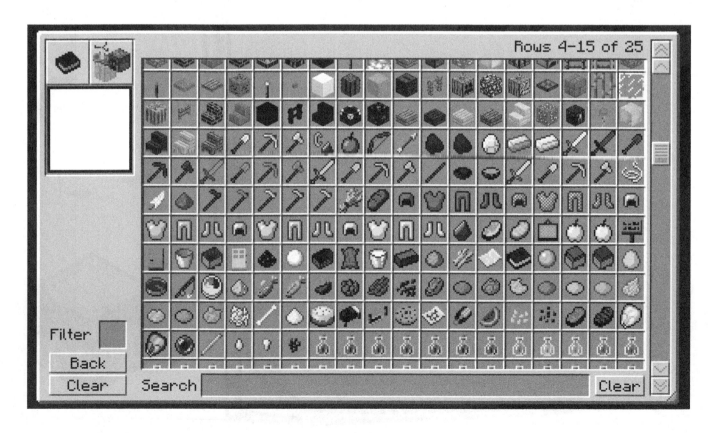

BRAIN GAMES

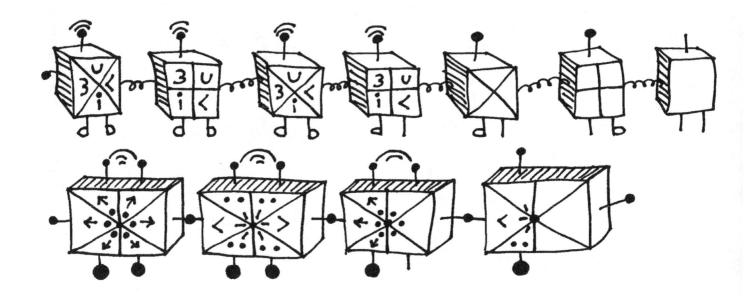

DRAW ANYTHING

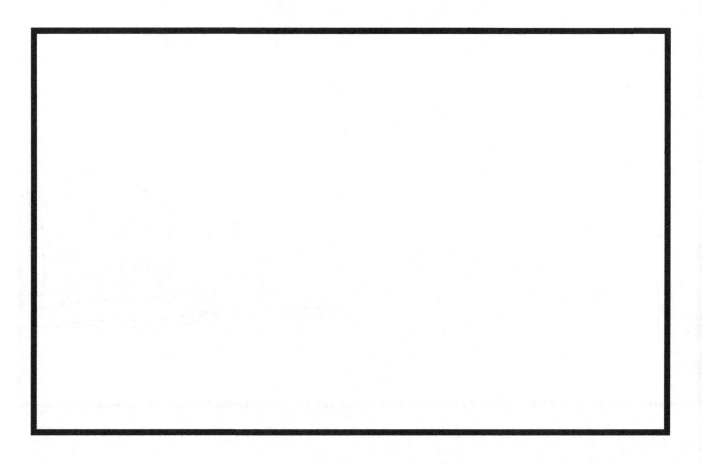

AN ANIMAL'S LIFE

TYPE OF ANIMAL:_____

BABY

HABITAT

FOOD

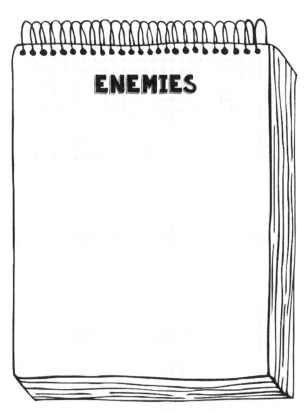

ENEMIES

MOVIE TIME

Watch an Educational Film, Tutorial or Documentary.

TITLE:_____

RATING:

Draw Your Favorite Scene:

Write a Review:

_____

_____

_____

_____

_____

MATH TIME

Use your math book or watch a math tutorial online. Use this graph paper for practice, lessons and notes.

WHat CaN YOU BuiLd?

 X7

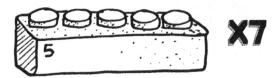 X7

 X7

 X7

 X7

 X7

Use seven of each kind of block.

What did you build?

_____

FINISH THE PICTURE

COMIC STRIP - WHAT HAPPENS NEXT ?

You are stuck in a deep ravine, your pickaxe is broken and all you have in your inventory is cobble stone, how do you get out?

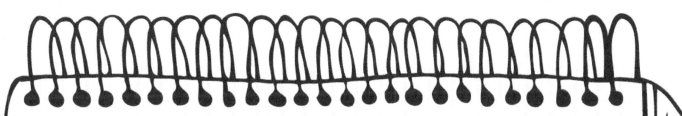

MINECRAFT FARMING

CHALLENGE
DRAW, DESIGN & BUILD

Design a horse barn. Build it in Minecraft.
Add horses to your barn.

CAN YOU MAKE IT?

Get a piece of origami paper and follow the instructions.

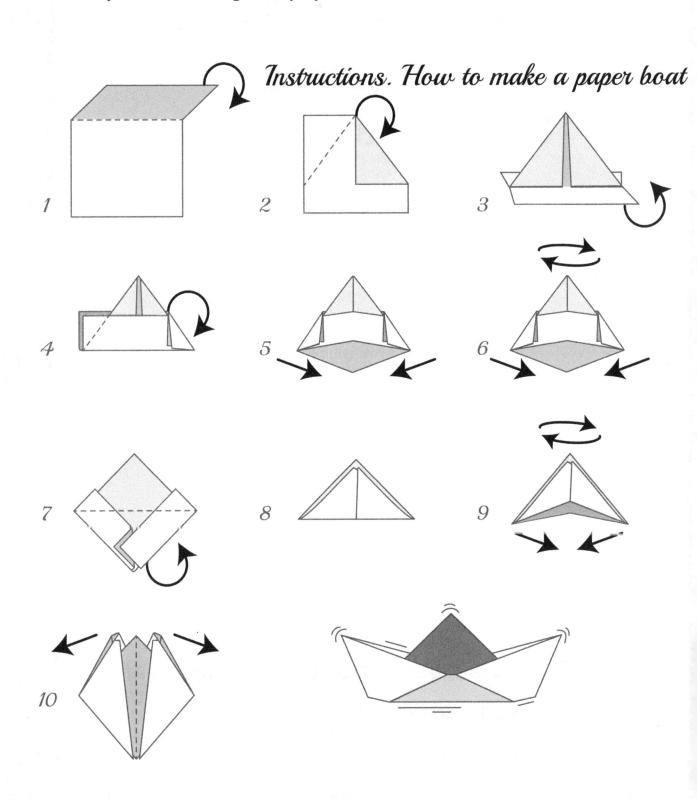

Instructions. How to make a paper boat

1
2
3
4
5
6
7
8
9
10

DIGITAL LETTERS

Create your own digital letters and numbers.

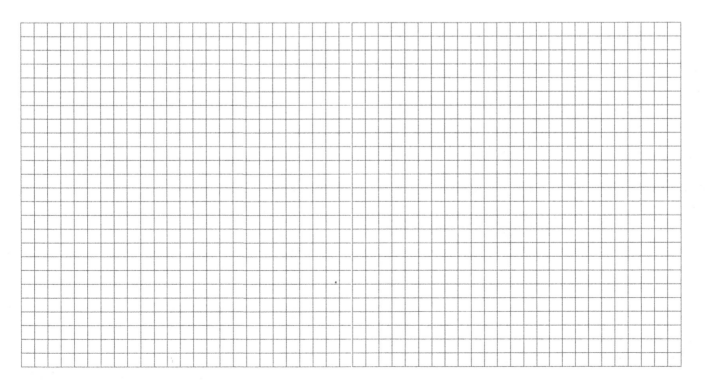

MONTH:

January

February

March

April

May

June

July

August

September

October

November

December

Pick an animal to learn about today, draw it:

_____

COLOR ME!

How are you
FEELING TODAY?

DAY:_____

_____

YEAR:_____

ANIMALS OF THE WORLD

What animal are you learning about?

_____

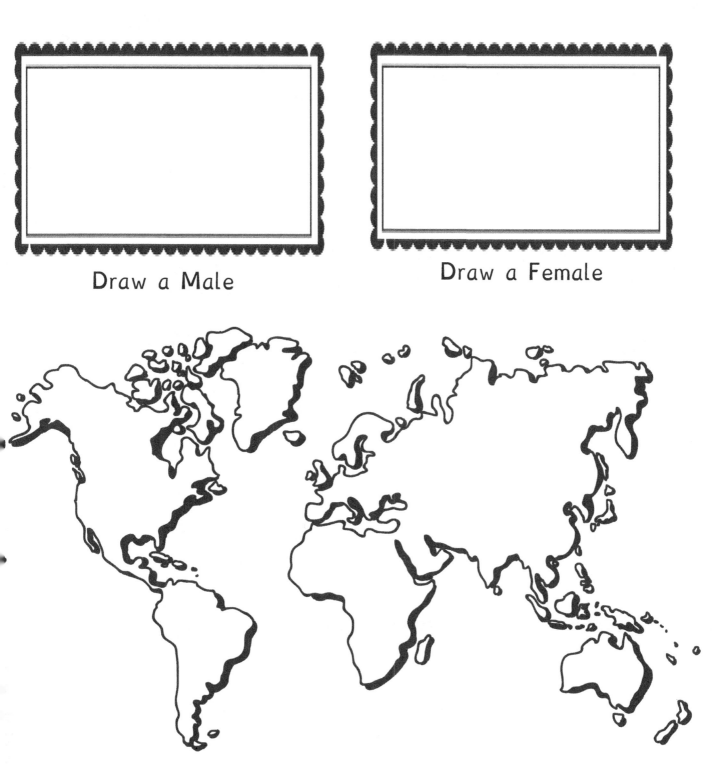

Draw a Male

Draw a Female

Color the parts of the world where this animal lives.

READING TIME

Write and draw about what you are learning.

BACKYARD SCIENCE
NATURE WALK & NATURE STUDY

Draw or write about the things you see outside today.

MATH PRACTICE

Check Your Work
with a Calculator

15 x 2	10 + 22
40 x 2	12 + 65
15 x 3	70 + 21
26 x 2	30 + 11
18 x 3	50 + 12

CIRCLE THE ITEMS

That Match Each Answer

289 − 5	210 + 54
345 + 10	301 − 12
604 − 300	304 + 66
200 + 67	488 − 150
700 − 344	234 + 79

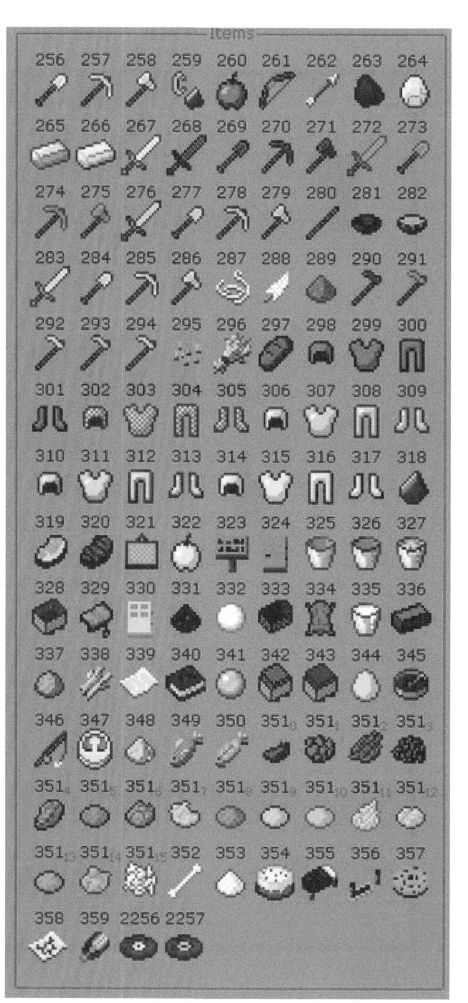

BRAIN GAMES

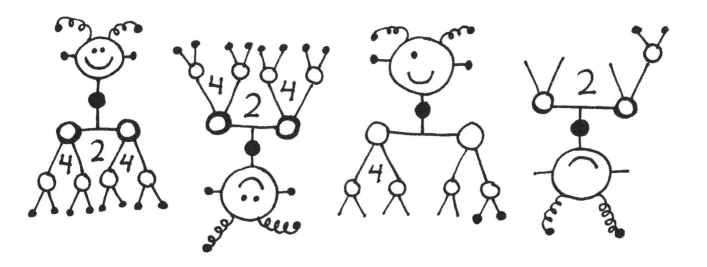

DRAW ANYTHING

CORE SUBJECTS - LEARNING TIME

Read ＿＿ pages in Your Science, Social Studies

& History Books. Write, Draw & Copy Important Information.

SCIENCE NOTES:

HISTORY NOTES:

SOCIAL STUDIES NOTES:

THE MOST INTERESTING THING I LEARNED:

SPELLING TIME

WORD HUNT

Choose A Letter

____

Find 10 words that include this letter.

1._____

2._____

3._____

4._____

5._____

6._____

7._____

8._____

9._____

10._____

PIXEL ART

Ideas & Inspiration

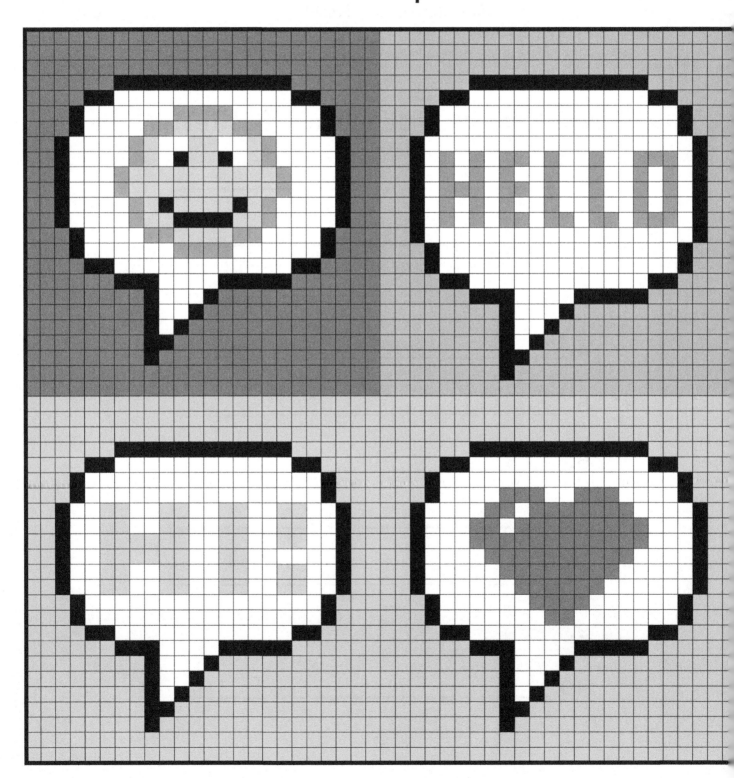

PIXEL ART

Create Your Own Pixel Design

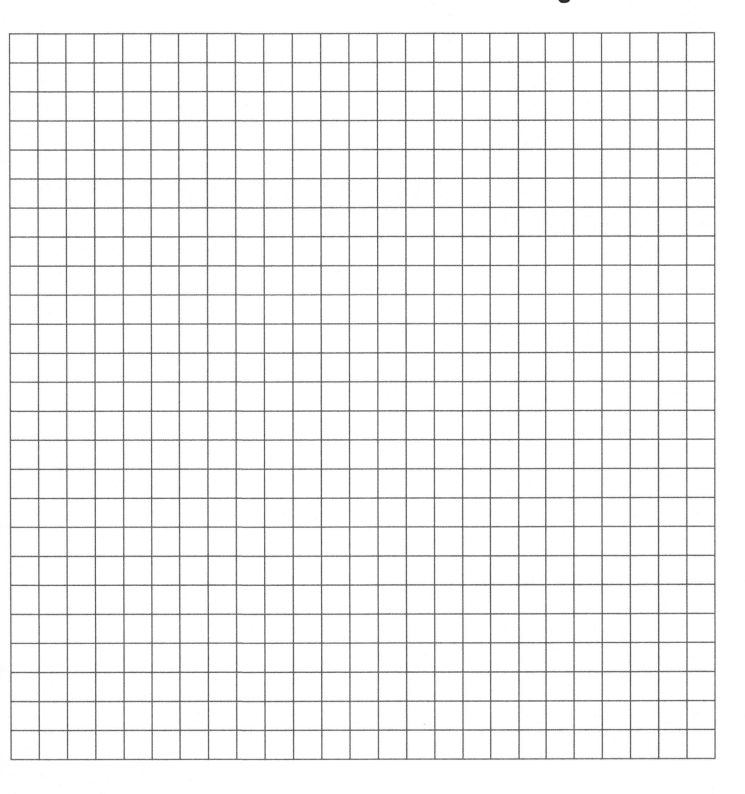

MONTH:

January

February

March

April

May

June

July

August

September

October

November

December

Pick an animal to learn about today, draw it:

_____

How are you
FEELING TODAY?

COLOR ME!

DAY:_____

_____

YEAR:_____

ART & LOGIC

Draw the Missing Parts

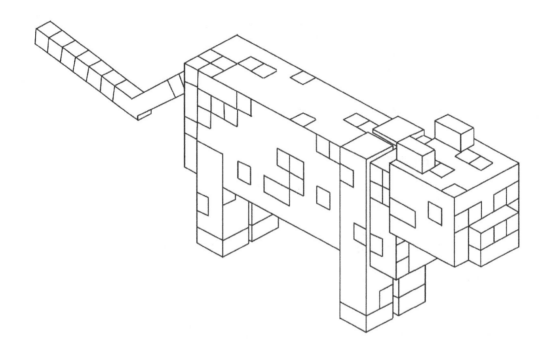

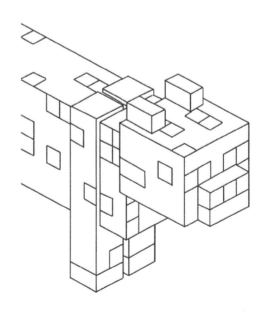

READING TIME

Write and draw about what you are learning.

BACKYARD SCIENCE
NATURE WALK & NATURE STUDY

Draw or write about the things you see outside today.

WHat CaN YOU BuiLd?

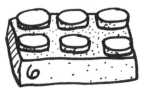 X7

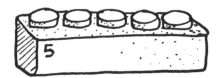 X7

 X7

 X7

 X7

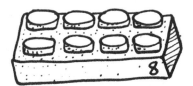 X7

 X7

Use seven of each kind of block.

What did you build?

_____

FiNiSH the Picture

BRAIN GAMES

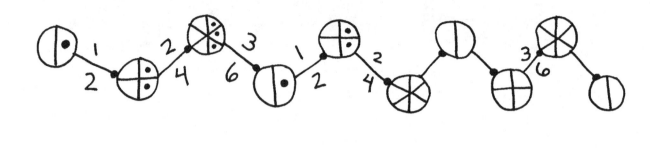

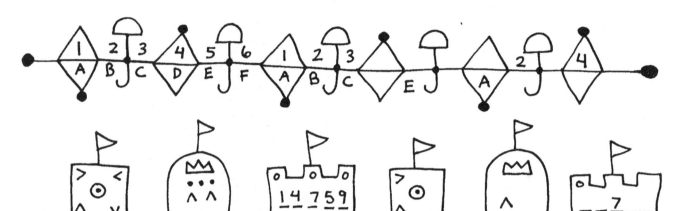

DRAW ANYTHING

Talk to someone about the difference
between real sheep and Minecraft sheep.

SPELLING TIME

WORD HUNT

Choose A Letter

_ _ _ _

Find 10 words that include this letter.

1._____

2._____

3._____

4._____

5._____

6._____

7._____

8._____

9._____

10._____

ANIMALS OF THE WORLD

What animal are you learning about?

_____

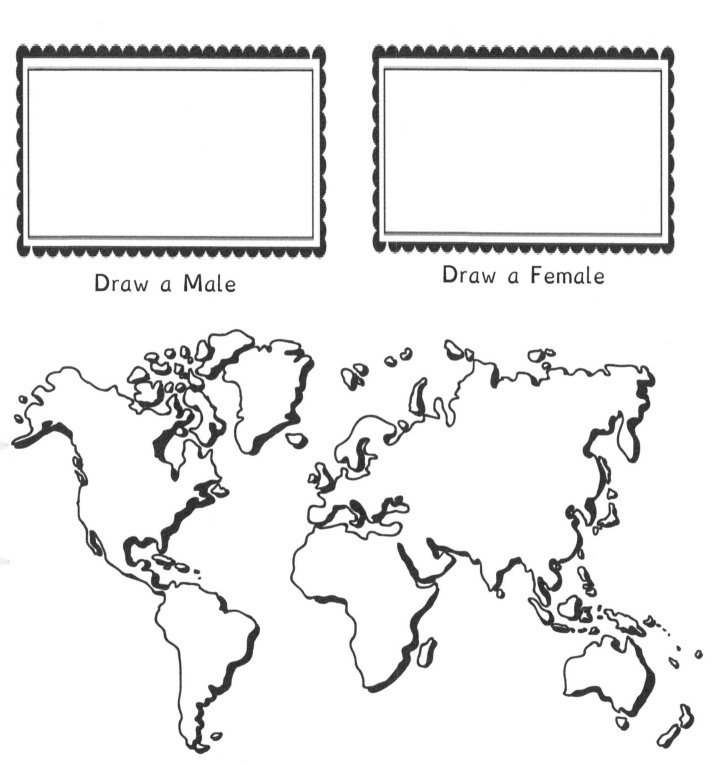

Draw a Male   Draw a Female

Color the parts of the world where this animal lives.

CREATE YOUR OWN CRAFTING RECIPE

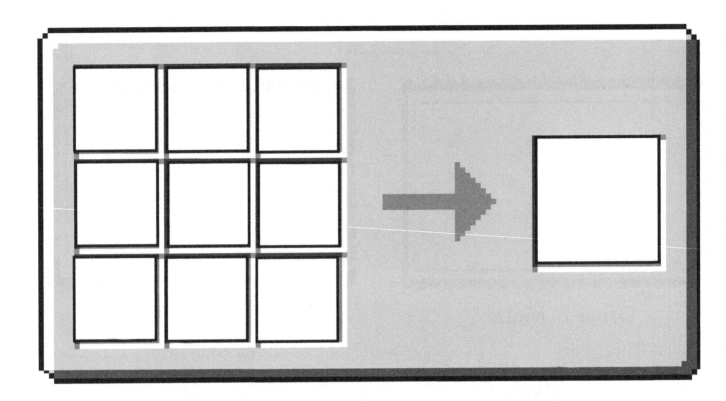

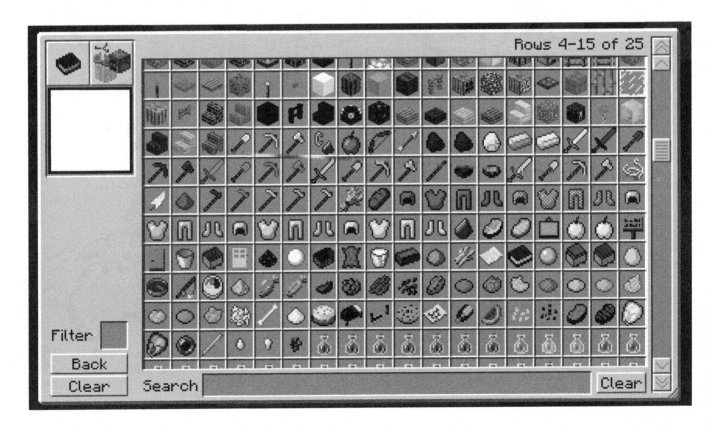

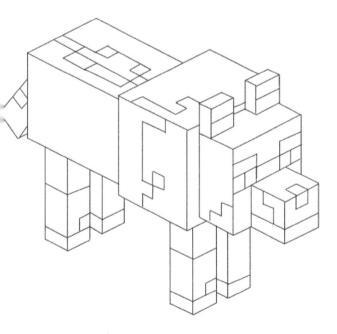

MOVIE TIME

Watch an Educational Film, Tutorial or Documentary.

TITLE:_____

RATING:

Draw Your Favorite Scene:

Write a Review:

_____

_____

_____

_____

_____

MATH TIME

Use your math book or watch a math
tutorial online. Use this graph paper for
practice, lessons and notes.

MONTH:

January

February

March

April

May

June

July

August

September

October

November

December

POETRY CORNER
Farm the Field (Tyburn Poem)

Hoeing
Plowing
Growing
Cooking
Clear off the land, hoeing, plowing.
Eat the good food, growing, cooking.

COLOR ME!

How are you
FEELING TODAY?

DAY:_____

_____

YEAR:_____

BACKYARD SCIENCE
NATURE WALK & NATURE STUDY

Draw or write about the things you see outside today.

READING TIME

Write and draw about what you are learning.

_____
_____
_____
_____
_____
_____
_____
_____

COPYWORK

Copy a sentence from one of your library books.

TITLE: _____Page#_____

_____

_____

_____

_____

DRAWING TIME

Copy an illustration from one of your books.

BRAIN GAMES

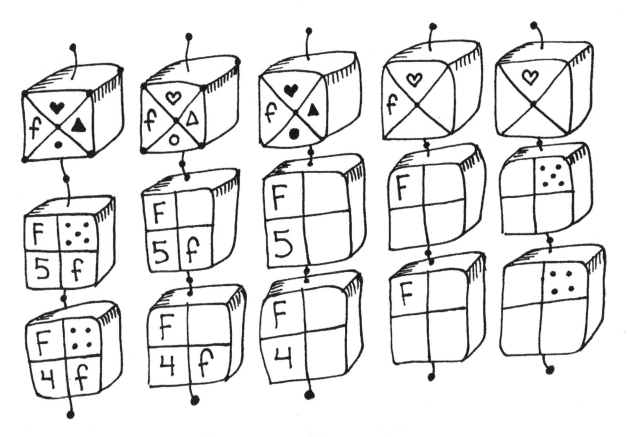

DRAW ANYTHING

Talk to someone about the difference between real chickens and Minecraft chickens.

MATH TIME

Use your math book or watch a math tutorial online. Use this graph paper for practice, lessons and notes.

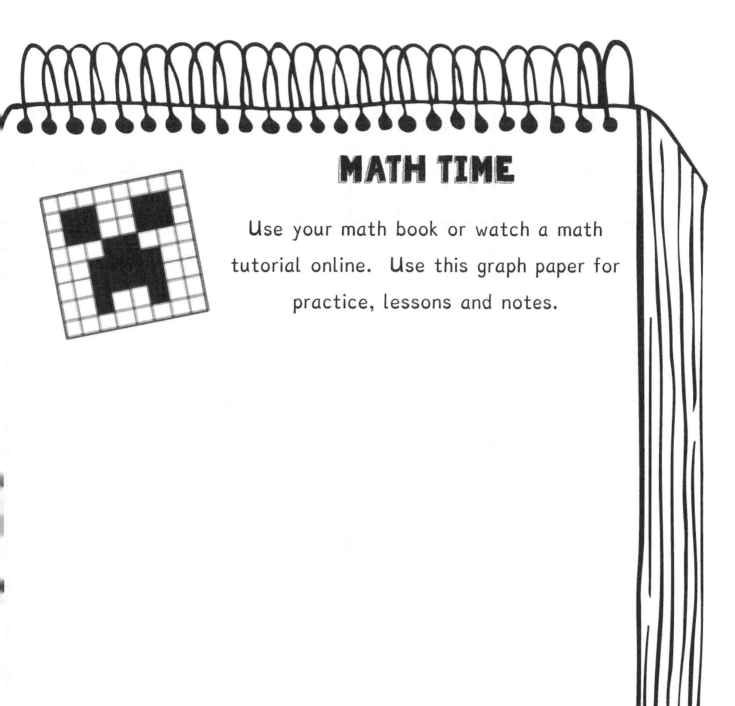

BRAIN GAMES

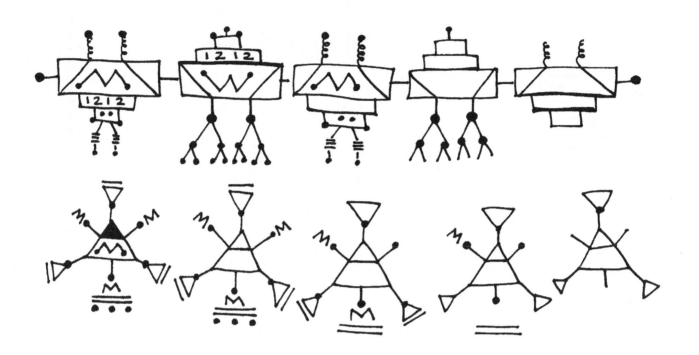

DRAW ANYTHING

JUST FOR FUN!

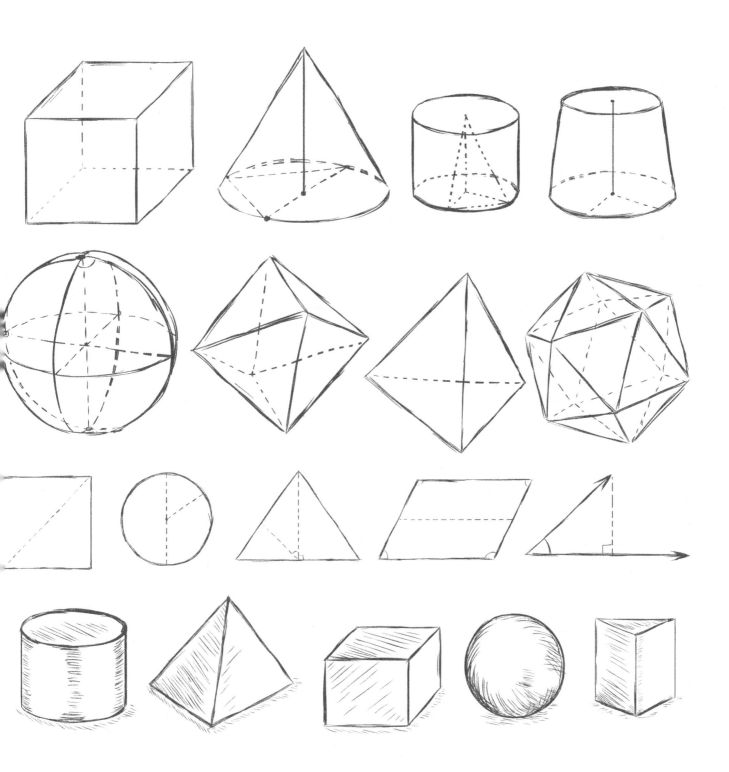

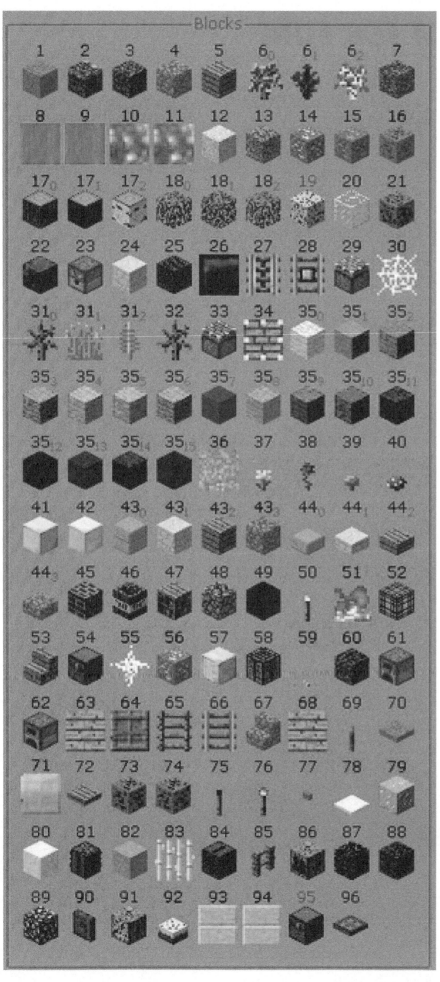

MATH PRACTICE

Check Your Work
with a Calculator

16	10
X 2	X 3
42	12
X 2	X 4
17	35
X 3	X 2
20	38
X 2	X 2
24	23
X 3	X 2

CIRCLE THE ITEMS

That Match Each Answer

289 − 10	310 − 54
345 − 20	301 − 40
700 − 350	404 − 96
407 − 77	388 − 50
611 − 244	543 − 199

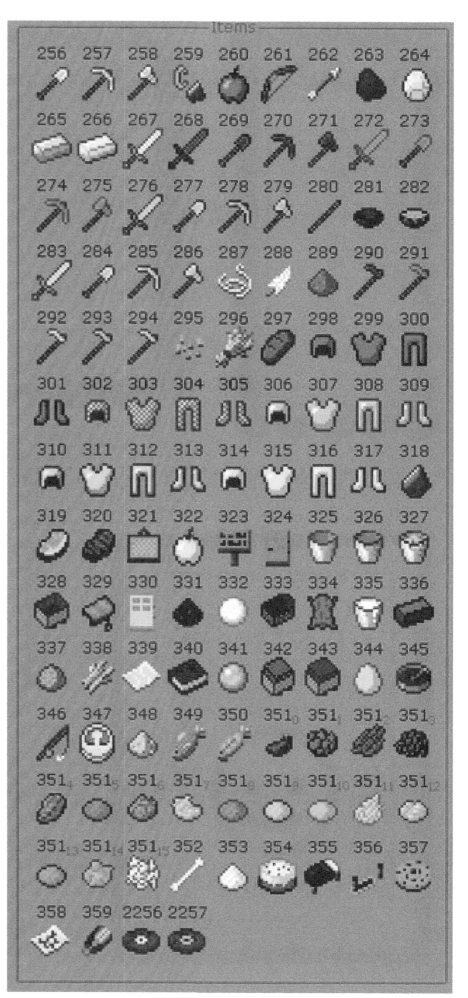

MONTH:
January

February

March

April

May

June

July

August

September

October

November

December

Pick an animal to learn about today, draw it:

_____

How are you FEELING TODAY?

COLOR ME!

DAY:_____

_____

YEAR:_____

LISTENING TIME
CLASSICAL MUSIC, HISTORY & LITERATURE

Listen to Story of the World, an audio book

or classical music. Draw and doodle below.

I am listening to: _____

CREATE YOUR OWN CRAFTING RECIPE

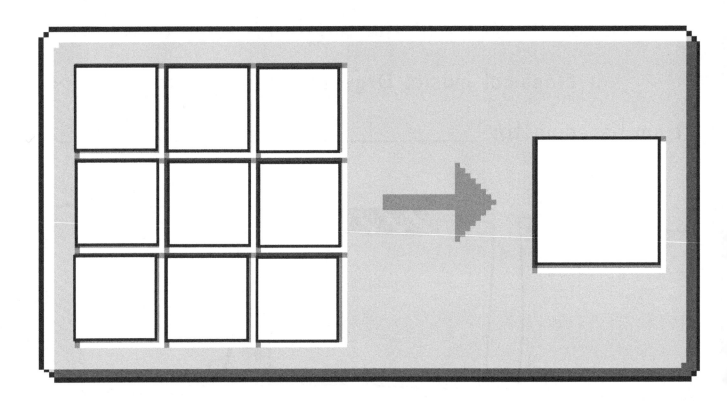

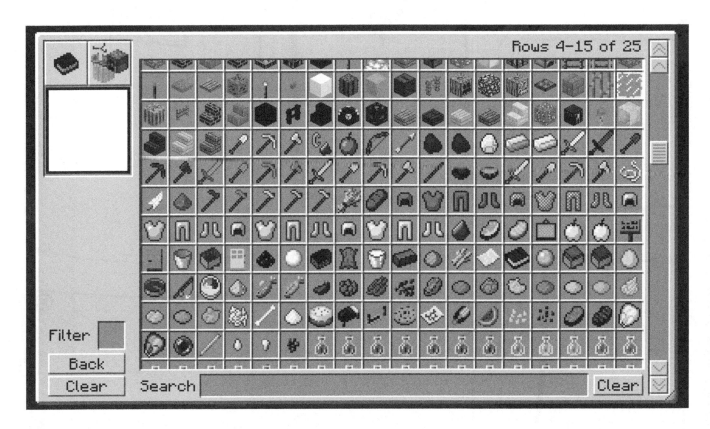

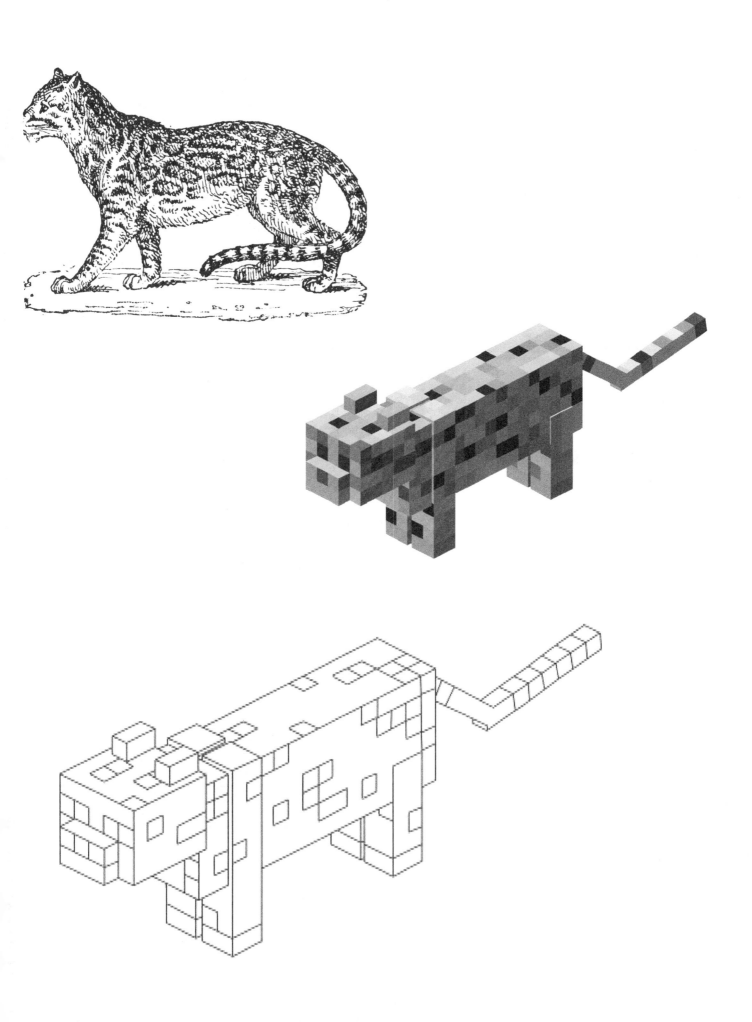

READING TIME

Write and draw about what you are learning.

BACKYARD SCIENCE
NATURE WALK & NATURE STUDY

Draw or write about the things you see outside today.

JUST FOR FUN!

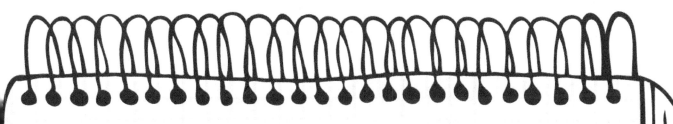

MINECRAFT FARMING

CHALLENGE
DRAW, DESIGN & BUILD

Draw a grain bin.

Build it in your Minecraft world.

AN ANIMAL'S LIFE
TYPE OF ANIMAL:_____

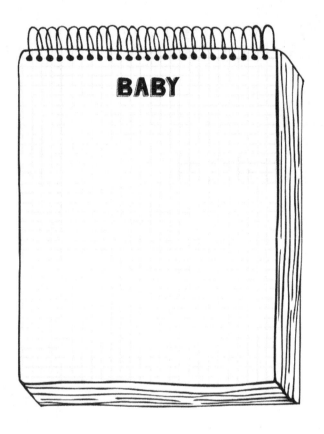

BABY

HABITAT

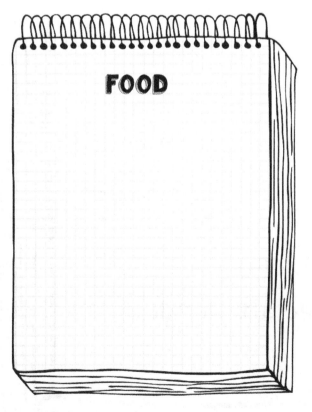

FOOD

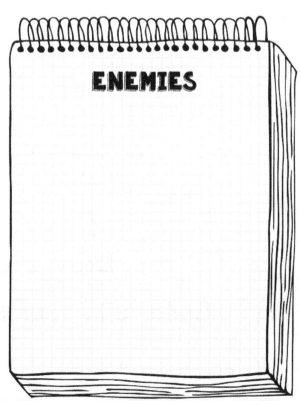

ENEMIES

BRAIN GAMES

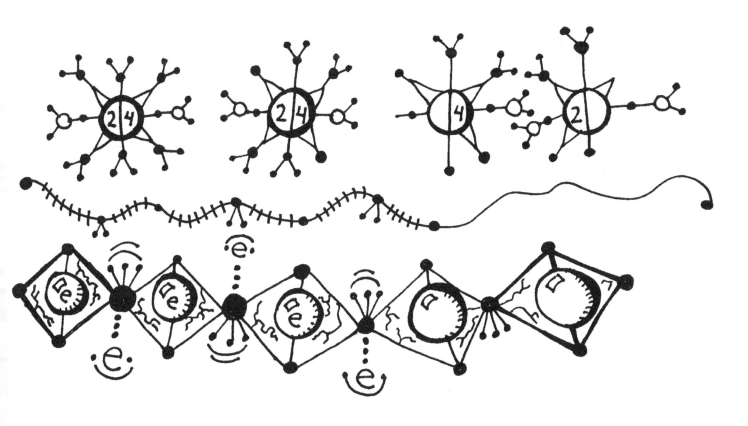

DRAW ANYTHING

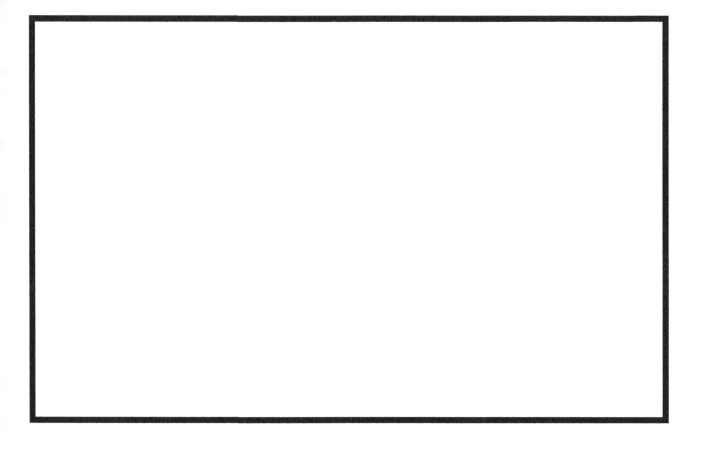

What Can YOU Build?

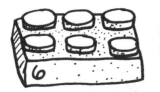 X6

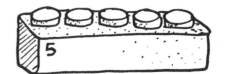 X6

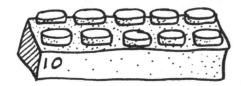 X6

 X6

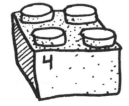 X6

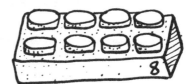 X6

 X6

Use six of each kind of block.

What did you build?

_____

FiNiSH the PictURe

DESIGN YOUR OWN SKIN

You and your friend were walking through a cave. All you have in your inventory is a diamond pickaxe, a water bucket, six carrots and full iron armor when........

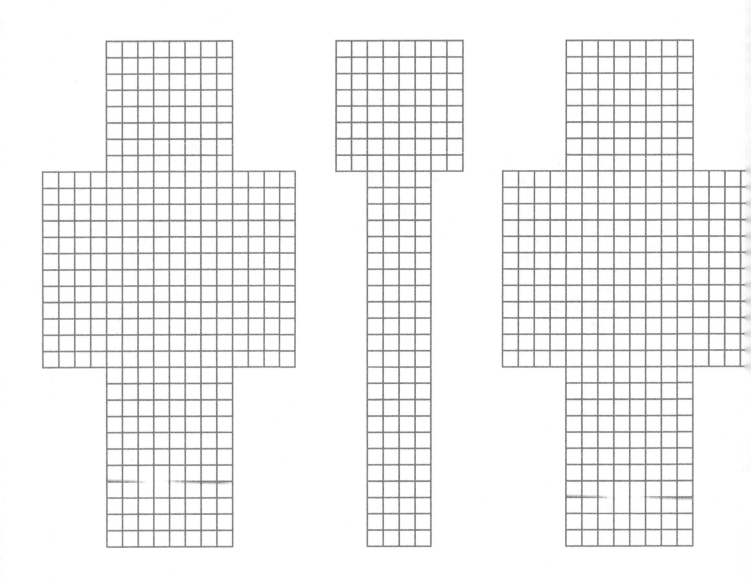

COPYWORK

Copy a sentence from one of your library books.

TITLE: _____Page#_____

_____

_____

_____

_____

DRAWING TIME

Copy an illustration from one of your books.

MOVIE TIME

Watch an Educational Film, Tutorial or Documentary.

TITLE:_____

RATING:

Draw Your Favorite Scene:

Write a Review:

_____
_____
_____
_____
_____

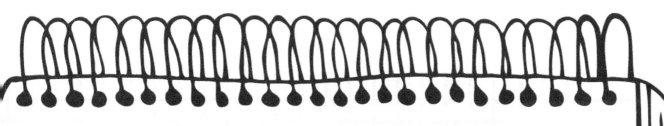

MATH TIME

Use your math book or watch a math tutorial online. Use this graph paper for practice, lessons and notes.

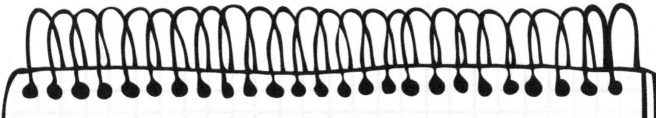

MINECRAFT FARMING

CHALLENGE
DRAW, DESIGN & BUILD

BUILD A ROLLER COASTER

Draw or Describe it Here:

COMIC STRIP - WHAT HAPPENS NEXT ?

You are deep in a cave, you found diamonds, but you can see lava dripping from above. What do you do?

MONTH:

January

February

March

April

May

June

July

August

September

October

November

December

Pick an animal to learn about today, draw it:

_____

COLOR ME!

How are you FEELING TODAY?

DAY:_____

_____

YEAR:_____

ANIMALS OF THE WORLD

What animal are you learning about?

_____

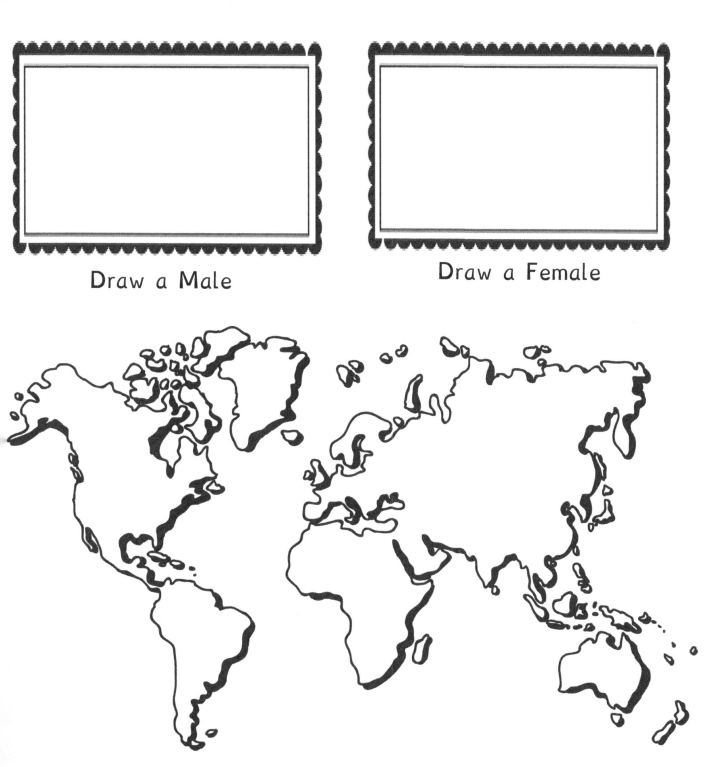

Draw a Male

Draw a Female

Color the parts of the world where this animal lives.

READING TIME

Write and draw about what you are learning.

BACKYARD SCIENCE
NATURE WALK & NATURE STUDY

Draw or write about the things you see outside today.

ART & LOGIC

Draw the Missing Parts

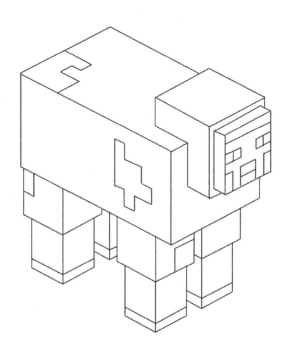
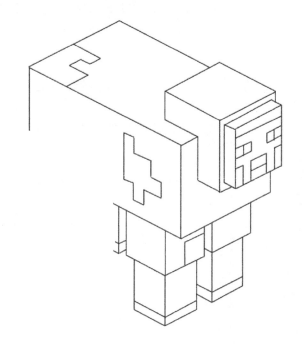
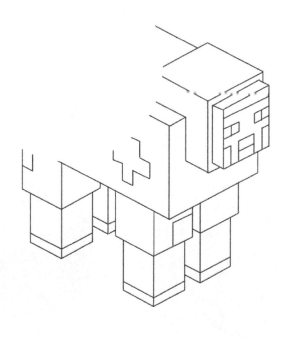
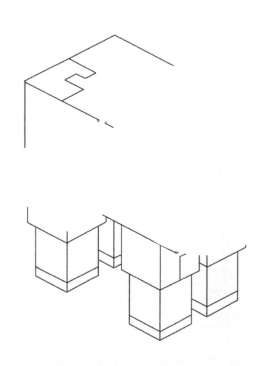

COMIC STRIP - WHAT HAPPENS NEXT ?

TITLE:_____

BRAIN GAMES

DRAW ANYTHING

Talk to someone about the difference between real horses and Minecraft horses.

CREATE YOUR OWN CRAFTING RECIPE

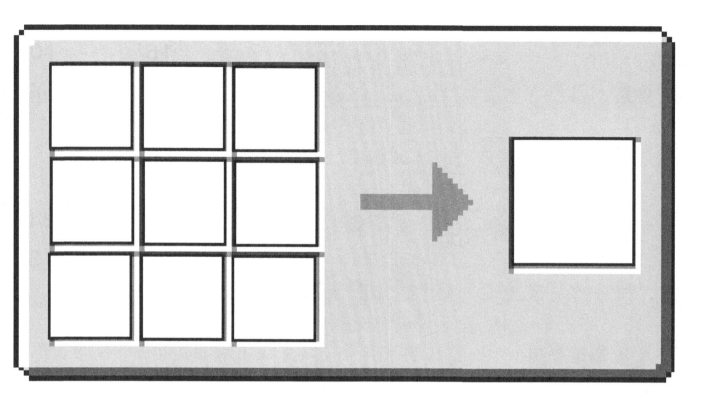

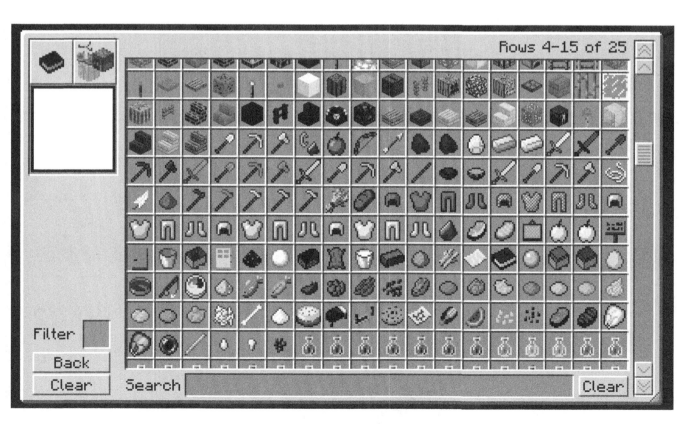

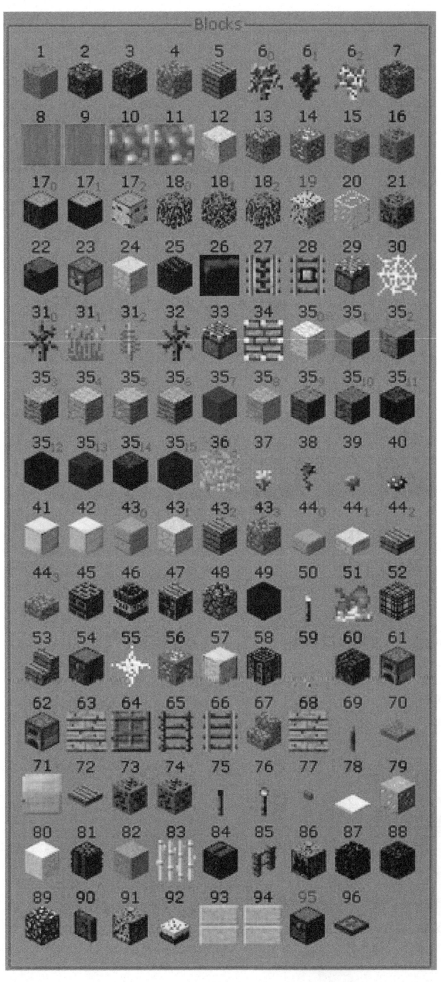

Blocks

MATH PRACTICE

Check Your Work
with a Calculator

16	10
x 3	x 4

22	24
x 3	x 3

18	30
x 3	x 2

30	31
x 3	x 2

11	12
x 3	x 4

CIRCLE THE ITEMS

That Match Each Answer

289 − 12	310 − 55
345 − 22	301 − 39
700 − 355	408 − 89
401 − 79	378 − 50
621 − 344	543 − 209

WHat CaN YOU BuiLd?

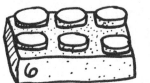 X3

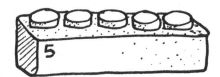 X3

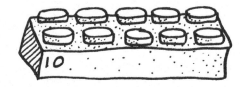 X3

 X3

 X3

 X3

 X3

Use three of each kind of block.

What did you build?

_____

FiNiSH tHe PiCtURe

CREATE YOUR OWN CRAFTING RECIPE

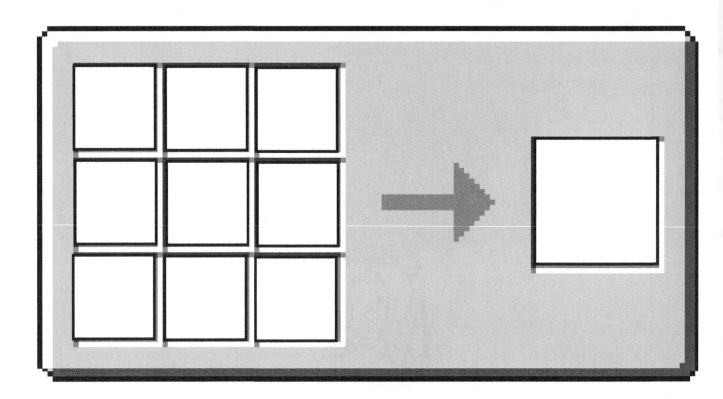

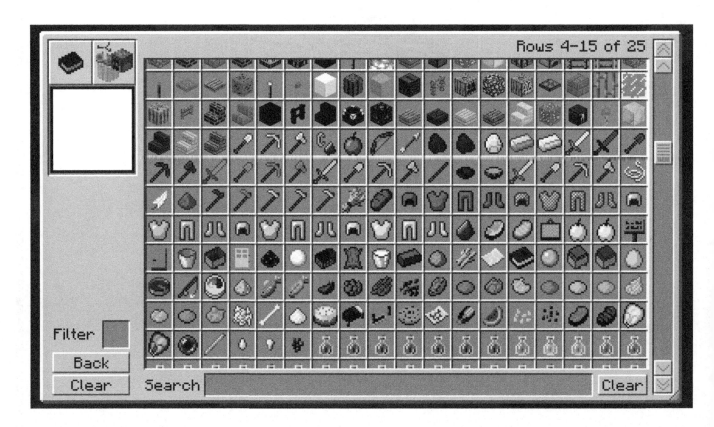

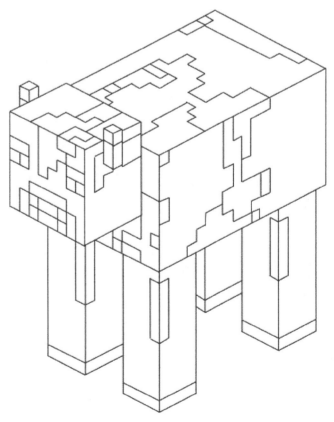

MONTH:

January

February

March

April

May

June

July

August

September

October

November

December

Pick an animal to learn about today, draw it:

_____

COLOR ME!

How are you
FEELING TODAY?

DAY:_____

_____

YEAR:_____

ART & LOGIC

Draw the Missing Parts

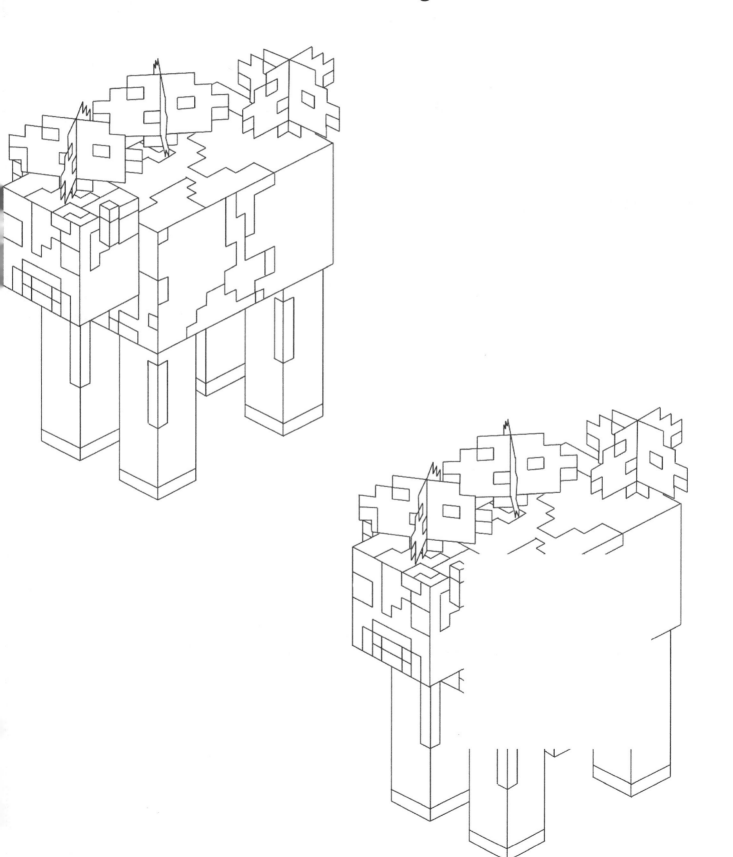

READING TIME

Write and draw about what you are learning.

BACKYARD SCIENCE
NATURE WALK & NATURE STUDY

Draw or write about the things you see outside today.

DESIGN YOUR OWN SKIN

You and your friend were walking through a cave. All you have in your inventory is a diamond pickaxe, a water bucket, six carrots and full iron armor when.........

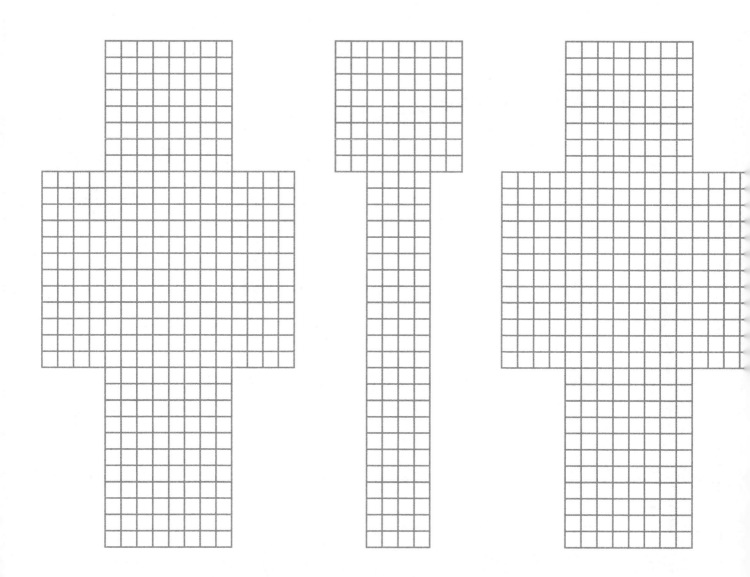

COMIC STRIP - WHAT HAPPENS NEXT ?

Create a comic strip to illustrate your story.

SPELLING TIME

WORD HUNT

Choose A Letter

_ _ _ _

Find 10 words that include this letter.

1._____

2._____

3._____

4._____

5._____

6._____

7._____

8._____

9._____

10._____

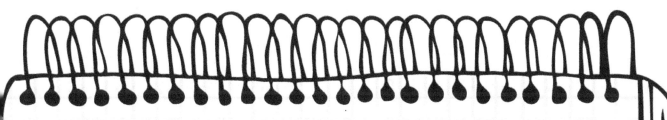

MINECRAFT FARMING

CHALLENGE
DRAW, DESIGN & BUILD

Design a rabbit hutch.

Build in your Minecraft world.

MOVIE TIME

Watch an Educational Film, Tutorial or Documentary.

TITLE:_____

RATING:

Draw Your Favorite Scene:

Write a Review:

_____

_____

_____

_____

_____

MATH TIME

Use your math book or watch a math tutorial online. Use this graph paper for practice, lessons and notes.

JUST FOR FUN!

ANIMALS OF THE WORLD

What animal are you learning about?

_____

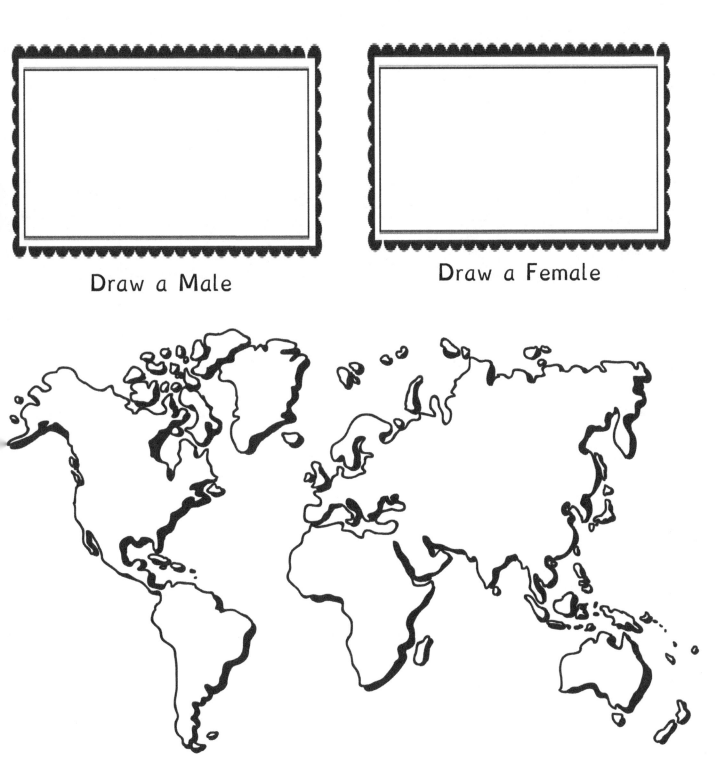

Draw a Male

Draw a Female

Color the parts of the world where this animal lives.

BRAIN GAMES

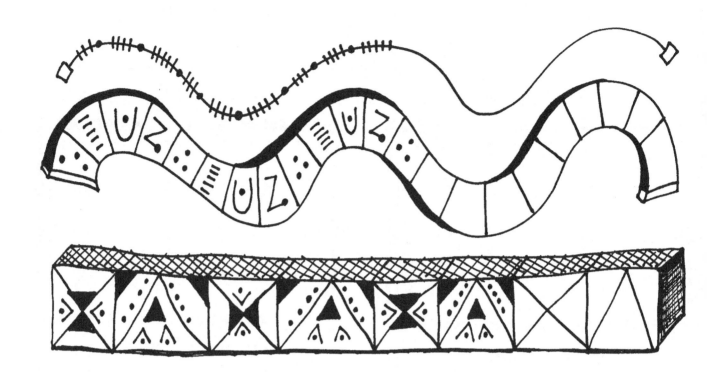

DRAW ANYTHING

Talk to someone about the difference between real pigs and Minecraft pigs.

CAN YOU MAKE IT?

Get a piece of origami paper and follow the instructions.

Instructions. How to make a paper airplane

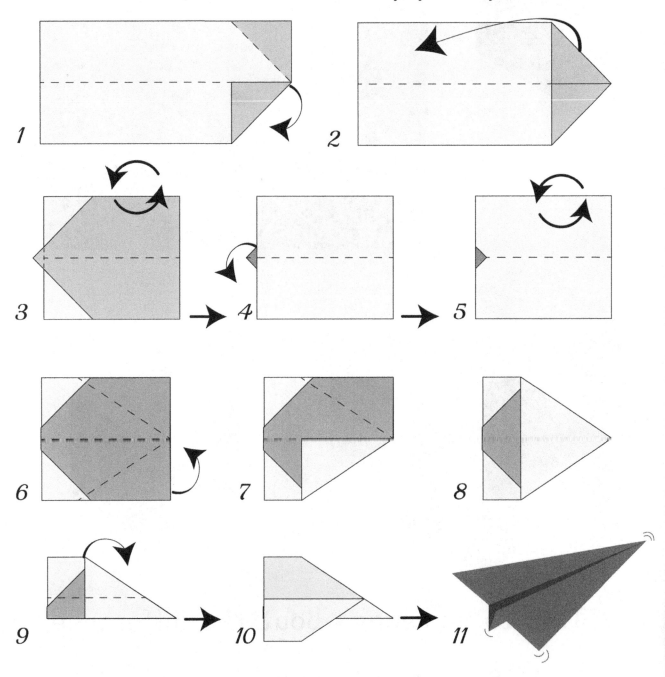

DIGITAL LETTERS

Create your own digital letters and numbers.

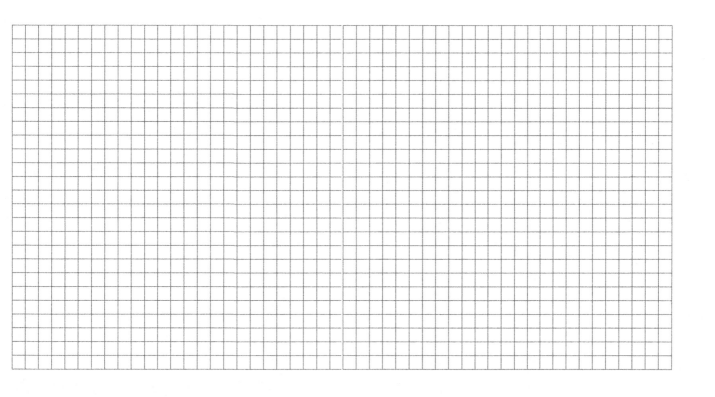

MONTH:

January

February

March

April

May

June

July

August

September

October

November

December

Pick an animal to learn about today, draw it:

_____

COLOR ME!

How are you FEELING TODAY?

DAY:_____

_____

YEAR:_____

BACKYARD SCIENCE
NATURE WALK & NATURE STUDY

Draw or write about the things you see outside today.

READING TIME

Write and draw about what you are learning.

COPYWORK

Copy a sentence from one of your library books.

TITLE: _____Page#_____

DRAWING TIME

Copy an illustration from one of your books.

WHat CaN YOU BuiLd?

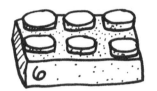 X4

 X4

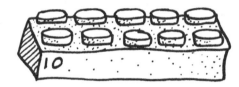 X4

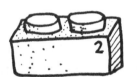 X4

 X4

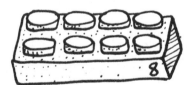 X4

 X4

Use four of each kind of block.

What did you build?

_____

FiNiSH tHe PictuRE

COMIC BOOK FONT WRITING PRACTICE

Try different comic book writing styles!

DYSLEXIE FONT BY CHRISTIAN BOER:

ABCDEFGHIJKLMNOPQRSTUVWXYZ

abcdefghijklmnopqrstuvwxyz

Create Your Own Font Here:

LISTENING TIME
CLASSICAL MUSIC, HISTORY & LITERATURE

Listen to Story of the World, an audio book

or classical music. Draw and doodle below.

I am listening to: _____

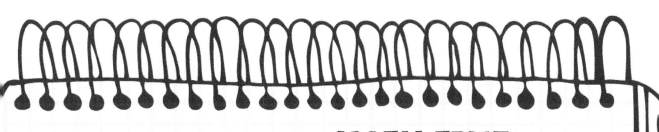

MATH TIME

Use your math book or watch a math tutorial online. Use this graph paper for practice, lessons and notes.

DESIGN YOUR OWN SKIN

You and your friend were walking through a cave. All you have in your inventory is a diamond pickaxe, a water bucket, six carrots and full iron armor when.........

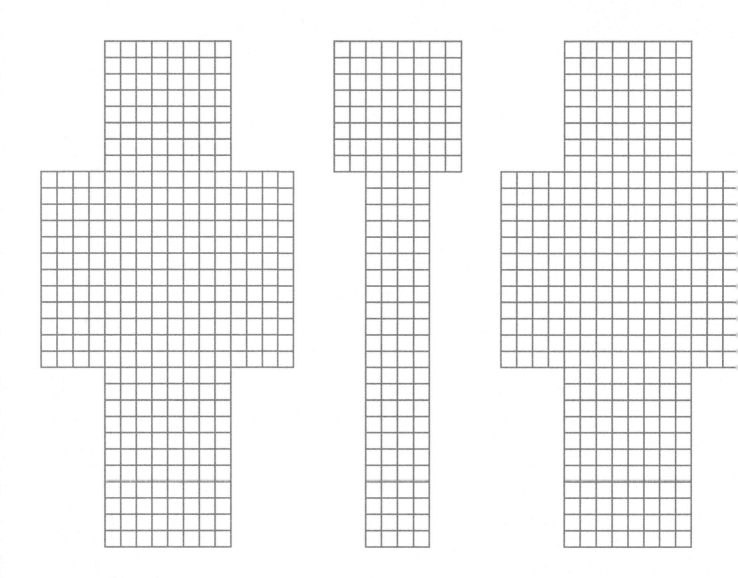

COMIC STRIP - WHAT HAPPENS NEXT ?

Create a comic strip to illustrate your story.

CREATE YOUR OWN CRAFTING RECIPE

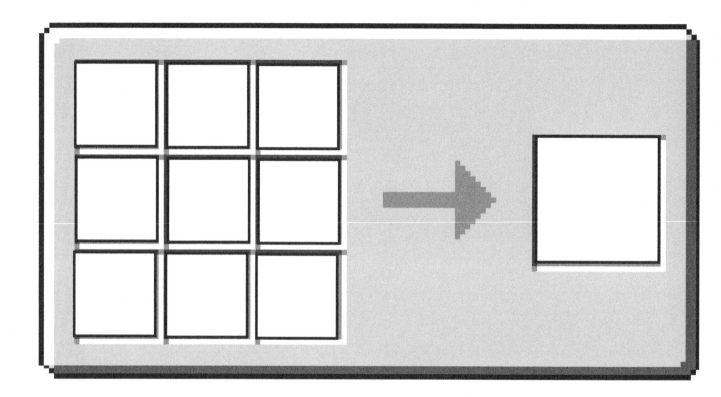

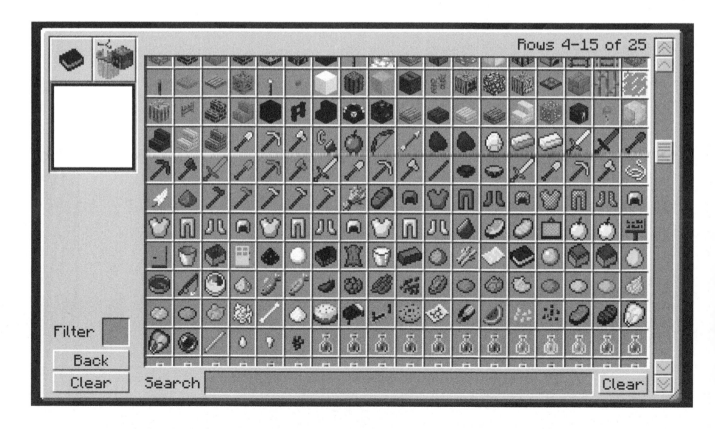

Filter

Back

Clear

Search

Clear

Talk to someone about farming, watch a video about farms.

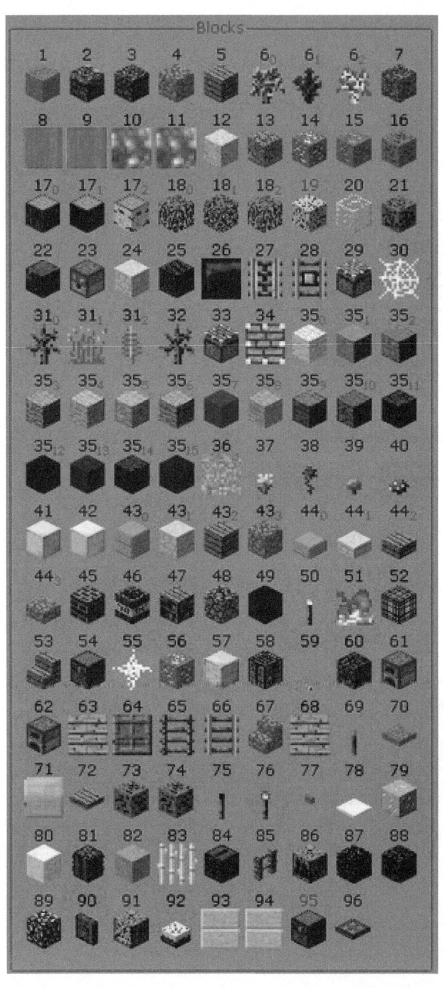

Blocks

MATH PRACTICE

Check Your Work
with a Calculator

20 x 3	10 x 5
20 x 4	25 x 3
15 x 3	18 x 4
30 x 3	15 x 4
40 x 2	13 x 4

CIRCLE THE ITEMS

That Match Each Answer

299 − 32	300 − 50
345 − 21	301 − 30
700 − 350	408 − 80
401 − 76	378 − 66
621 − 300	543 − 250

MONTH:

January

February

March

April

May

June

July

August

September

October

November

December

Pick an animal to learn about today, draw it:

_____

COLOR ME!

How are you
FEELING TODAY?

DAY:_____

_____

YEAR:_____

LISTENING TIME
CLASSICAL MUSIC, HISTORY & LITERATURE

Listen to Story of the World, an audio book

or classical music. Draw and doodle below.

I am listening to: _____

READING TIME

Write and draw about what you are learning.

BACKYARD SCIENCE
NATURE WALK & NATURE STUDY

Draw or write about the things you see outside today.

BRAIN GAMES

DRAW ANYTHING

DRAW THE CROPS YOU
CAN GROW IN MINECRAFT

JUST FOR FUN!

AN ANIMAL'S LIFE

TYPE OF ANIMAL:_____

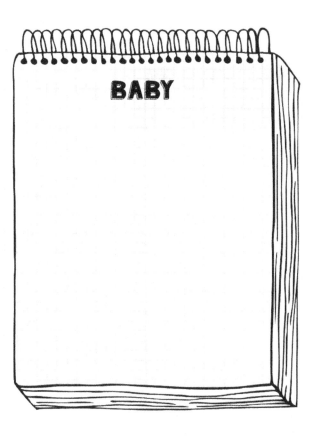

BABY

HABITAT

FOOD

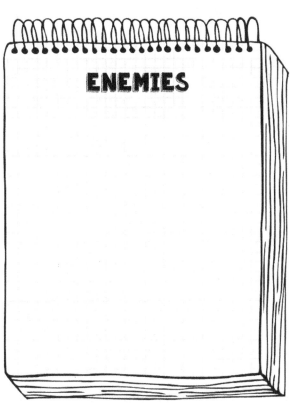

ENEMIES

MOVIE TIME

Watch an Educational Film, Tutorial or Documentary.

TITLE:_____

RATING:

Draw Your Favorite Scene:

Write a Review:

_____
_____
_____
_____
_____

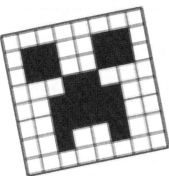

MATH TIME

Use your math book or watch a math tutorial online. Use this graph paper for practice, lessons and notes.

WHat CaN YOU BuiLd?

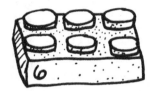 X5

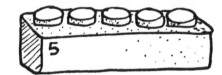 X5

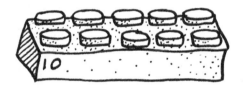 X5

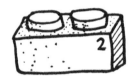 X5

 X5

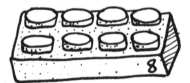 X5

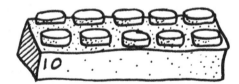 X5

 X5

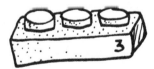 X5

Use five of each kind of block.

What did you build?

_____

FiNiSH tHe PictURe

MONTH:

January

February

March

April

May

June

July

August

September

October

November

December

Pick an animal to learn about today, draw it:

_____

COLOR ME!

How are you FEELING TODAY?

DAY:_____

_____

YEAR:_____

ANIMALS OF THE WORLD

What animal are you learning about?

_____

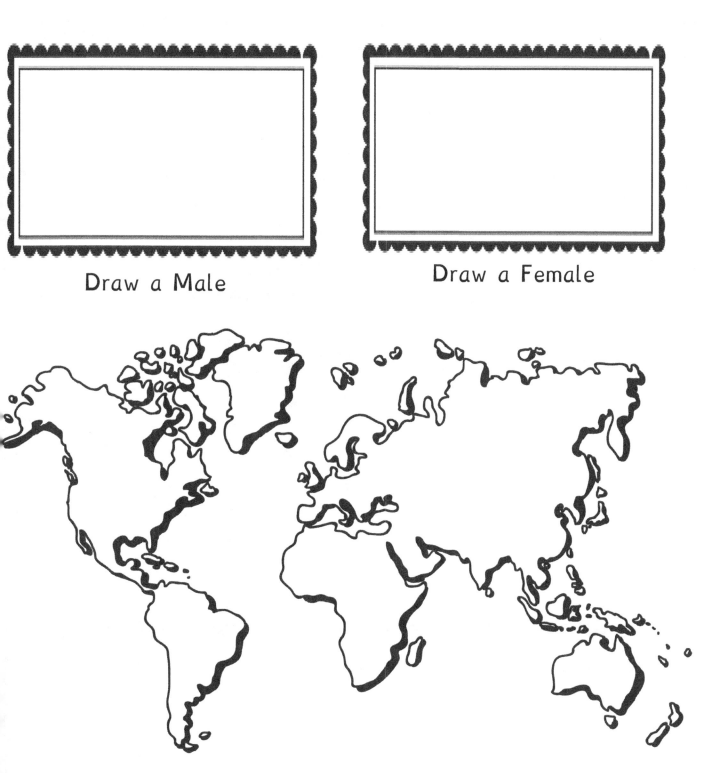

Draw a Male

Draw a Female

Color the parts of the world where this animal lives.

READING TIME

Write and draw about what you are learning.

BACKYARD SCIENCE
NATURE WALK & NATURE STUDY

Draw or write about the things you see outside today.

ART & LOGIC

Draw the Missing Parts

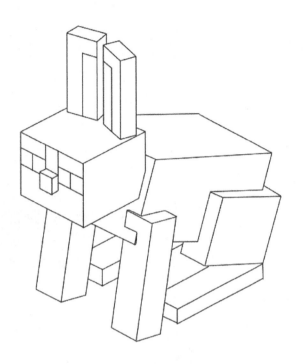

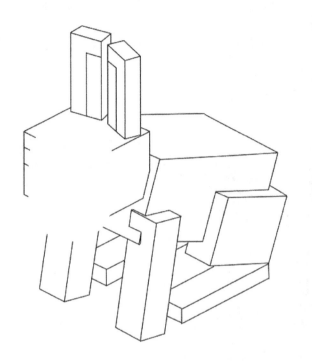

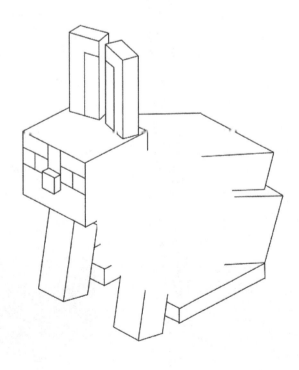

COMIC STRIP - WHAT HAPPENS NEXT ?

TITLE:_____

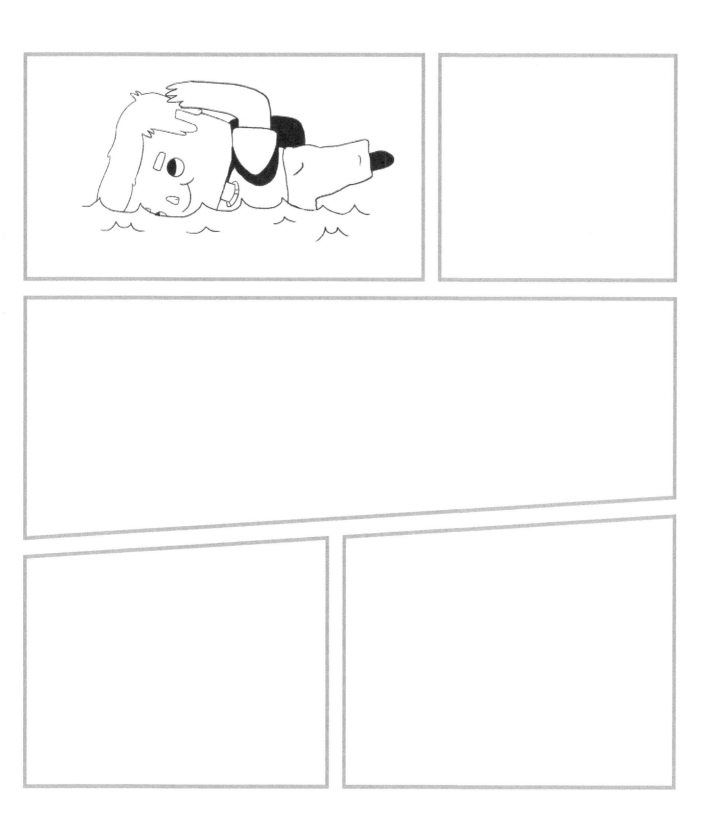

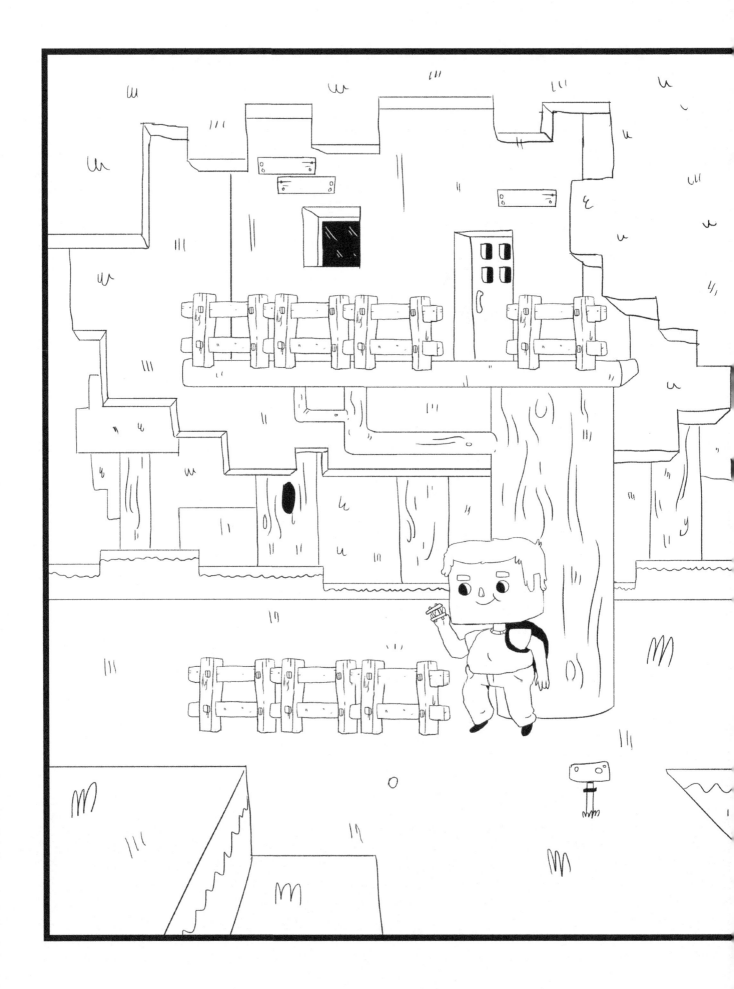

BRAIN GAMES

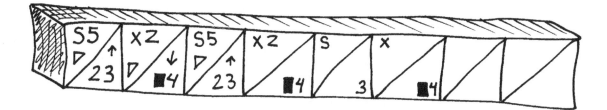

DRAW ANYTHING

CORE SUBJECTS - LEARNING TIME

Read __ pages in Your Science, Social Studies

& History Books. Write, Draw & Copy Important Information

SCIENCE NOTES:

HISTORY NOTES:

SOCIAL STUDIES NOTES:

THE MOST INTERESTING THING I LEARNED:

SPELLING TIME

WORD HUNT

Choose A Letter

_ _ _ _

Find 10 words that include this letter.

1._____

2._____

3._____

4._____

5._____

6._____

7._____

8._____

9._____

10._____

CREATE YOUR OWN CRAFTING RECIPE

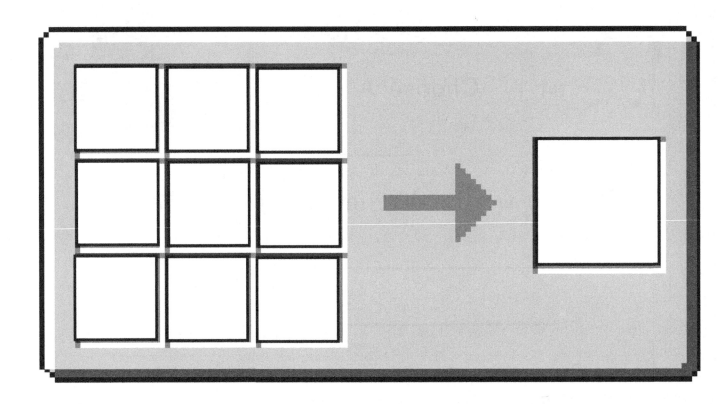

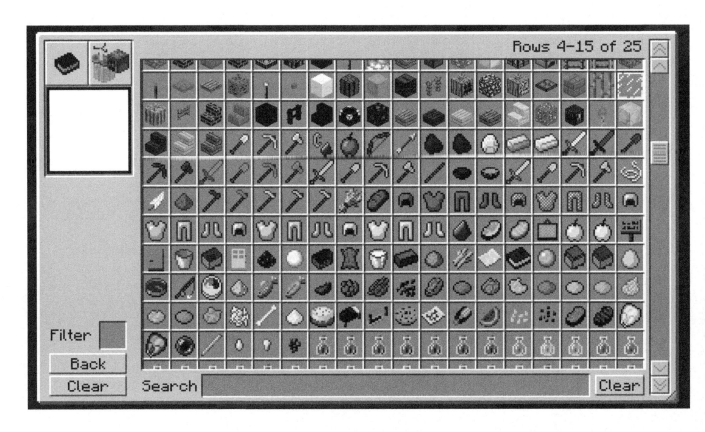

DRAW A FARM

MONTH:

January

February

March

April

May

June

July

August

September

October

November

December

Pick an animal to learn about today, draw it:

_____

COLOR ME!

How are you FEELING TODAY?

DAY:____

_____

YEAR:_____

YOU HAVE SEEN THIS ANIMAL ON MINECRAFT.
NOW DESIGN YOUR OWN ANIMAL.

READING TIME

Write and draw about what you are learning.

BACKYARD SCIENCE
NATURE WALK & NATURE STUDY

Draw or write about the things you see outside today.

PERIODIC TABLE OF ELEMENTS

Color the elements that exist both in the real world and in Minecraft.

1 **H** 1.0079 Hydrogen									

3 **Li** 1.941 Lithium	4 **Be** 9.0122 Beryllium

11 **Na** 22.990 Sodium	12 **Mg** 24.305 Magnesium

19 **K** 39.098 Potassium	20 **Ca** 40.078 Calcium	21 **Sc** 44.956 Scandium	22 **Ti** 47.867 Titanium	23 **V** 50.942 Vanadium	24 **Cr** 51.996 Chromium	25 **Mn** 54.938 Manganese	26 **Fe** 55.845 Iron	27 **Co** 58.933 Cobalt
37 **Rb** 85.468 Rubidium	38 **Sr** 87.62 Strontium	39 **Y** 88.906 Yttrium	40 **Zr** 91.224 Zirconium	41 **Nb** 92.906 Niobium	42 **Mo** 95.94 Molybdenum	43 **Tc** 98 Technetium	44 **Ru** 101.07 Ruthenium	45 **Rh** 102.91 Rhodium
55 **Cs** 132.91 Cesium	56 **Ba** 137.33 Barium	57 - 71 **La-Lu**	72 **Hf** 178.49 Hafnium	73 **Ta** 180.95 Tantalum	74 **W** 183.84 Tungsten	75 **Re** 186.21 Rhenium	76 **Os** 190.23 Osmium	77 **Ir** 192.22 Iridium
87 **Fr** 223 Francium	88 **Ra** 226 Radium	89 - 103 **Ac-Lr**	104 **Rf** 261 Rutherfordium	105 **Db** 262 Dubnium	106 **Sg** 266 Seaborgium	107 **Bh** 264 Bohrium	108 **Hs** 269 Hassium	109 **Mt** 268 Meitnerium

Lanthanide series

57 **La** 138.91 Lanthanide	58 **Ce** 140.12 Cerium	59 **Pr** 140.91 Praseodymium	60 **Nd** 144.24 Neodymium	61 **Pm** 145 Promethium	62 **Sm** 150.36 Samarium	63 **Eu** 151.96 Europium

Actinide series

89 **Ac** 227 Actinide	90 **Th** 232.04 Thorium	91 **Pa** 231.04 Protactinium	92 **U** 238.03 Uranium	93 **Np** 237 Neptunium	94 **Pu** 244 Plutonium	95 **Am** 243 Americium

USE THE COLORS AND TEXTURES
FOUND IN THE GAME.

2 He 4.0026 Helium

5 B 10.811 Boron	6 C 12.011 Carbon	7 N 14.007 Nitrogen	8 O 15.999 Oxygen	9 F 18.998 Fluorine	10 Ne 20.180 Neon
13 Al 26.982 Aluminium	14 Si 28.086 Silicon	15 P 30.974 Phosphorus	16 S 32.065 Sulfur	17 Cl 35.453 Chlorine	18 Ar 39.948 Argon

28 Ni 58.693 Nickel	29 Cu 63.546 Copper	30 Zn 65.39 Zinc	31 Ga 69.723 Gallium	32 Ge 1.0079 Germanium	33 As 74.992 Arsenic	34 Se 78.96 Selenium	35 Br 79.904 Bromine	36 Kr 83.80 Krypton
46 Pd 106.42 Palladium	47 Ag 107.87 Silver	48 Cd 112.41 Cadmium	49 In 114.82 Indium	50 Sn 118.71 Tin	51 Sb 121.76 Antimony	52 Te 127.60 Tellurium	53 I 126.90 Iodine	54 Xe 131.29 Xenon
78 Pt 195.08 Platinum	79 Au 196.97 Gold	80 Hg 200.59 Mercury	81 Tl 204.38 Thallium	82 Pb 207.2 Lead	83 Bi 208.98 Bismuth	84 Po 209 Polonium	85 At 210 Astatine	86 Rn 222 Radon
110 Uun 271 Ununnilium	111 Uuu 272 Unununium	112 Uub 1.0079 Ununbium	113 Uut Ununtrium	114 Uuq 289 Ununquadium	115 Uup Ununpentium	116 Uuh Ununhexium	117 Uus Ununseptium	118 Uuo Ununoctium

64 Gd 157.25 Gadolinum	65 Tb 158.93 Terbium	66 Dy 162.5 Dysprosium	67 Ho 164.93 Holmium	68 Er 1.0079 Erbium	69 Tm 168.93 Thulium	70 Yb 173.04 Yttersium	71 Lu 1.0079 Lutetium
96 Cm 247 Curium	97 Bk 247 Berkelium	98 Cf 251 Californium	99 Es 252 Einsteinium	100 Fm 257 Fermium	101 Md 258 Mendelevium	102 No 259 Nobelium	103 Lr 1.0079 Lawrencium

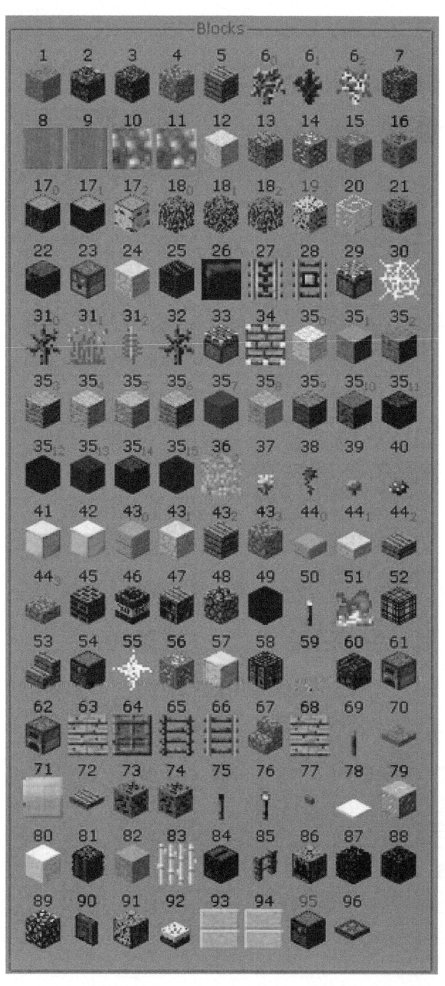

MATH PRACTICE

Check Your Work
with a Calculator

30 x 3	21 x 3
7 x 4	12 x 3
16 x 3	19 x 4
22 x 3	17 x 4
13 x 4	19 x 4

CIRCLE THE ITEMS

That Match Each Answer

299 + 12	300 + 50
345 + 21	301 + 40
10 + 340	208 + 80
222 + 76	234 + 55
121 + 200	143 + 150

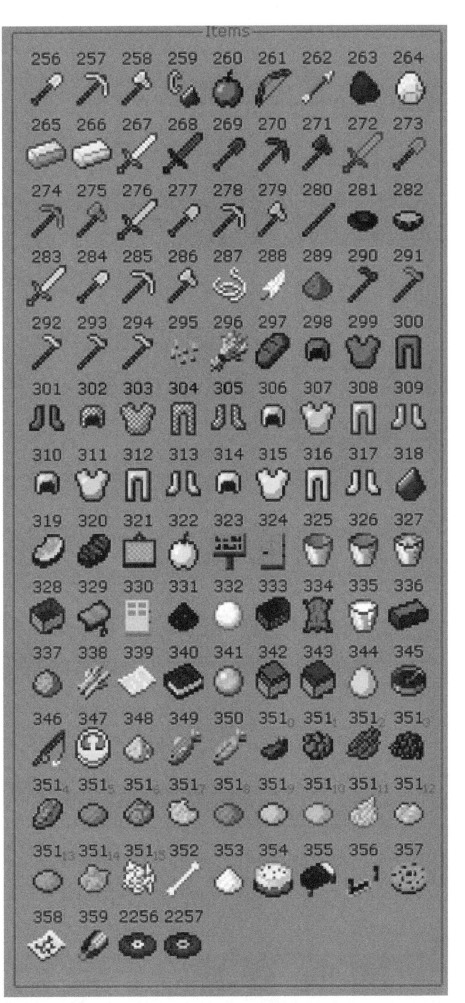

MOVIE TIME

Watch an Educational Film, Tutorial or Documentary.

TITLE:_____

Draw Your Favorite Scene:

RATING

Write a Review:

_____

_____

_____

_____

_____

MATH TIME

Use your math book or watch a math tutorial online. Use this graph paper for practice, lessons and notes.

CREATE YOUR OWN CRAFTING RECIPE

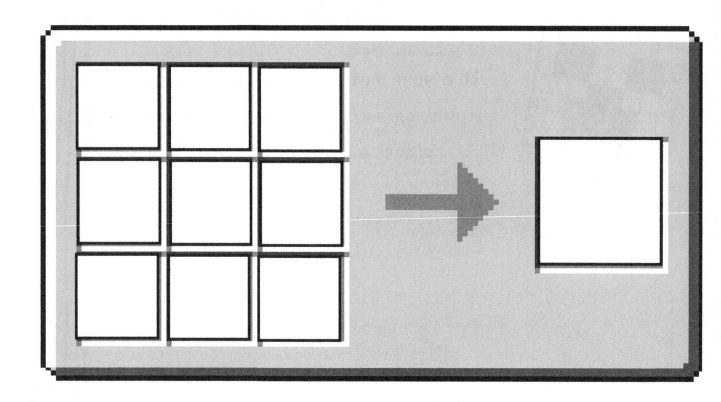

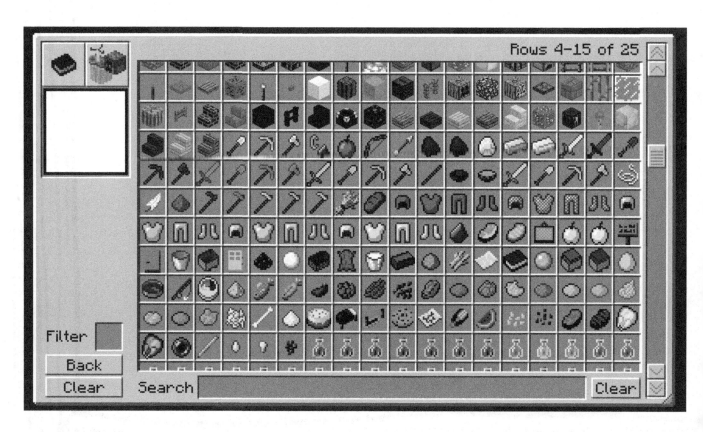

BRAIN GAMES

DRAW ANYTHING

DESIGN YOUR OWN SKIN

You and your friend were walking through a cave. All you have in your inventory is a diamond pickaxe, a water bucket, six carrots and full iron armor when.........

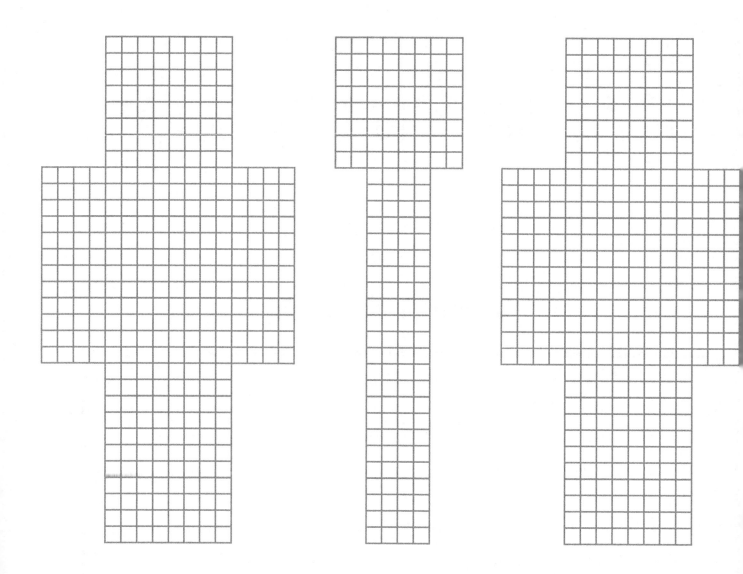

COMIC STRIP - WHAT HAPPENS NEXT ?

Create a comic strip to illustrate your story.

MONTH:

January

February

March

April

May

June

July

August

September

October

November

December

Pick an animal to learn about today, draw it:

_____

COLOR ME!

How are you
FEELING TODAY?

DAY:_____

_____

YEAR:_____

BACKYARD SCIENCE
NATURE WALK & NATURE STUDY

Draw or write about the things you see outside today.

READING TIME

Write and draw about
what you are learning.

COPYWORK

Copy a sentence from one of your library books.

TITLE: _____Page#_____

DRAWING TIME

Copy an illustration from one of your books.

WHAT CaN YOU BuiLd?

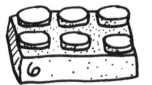 **X3**

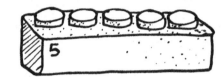 **X3**

 **X3**

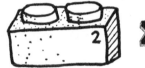 **X3**

 **X3**

 **X3**

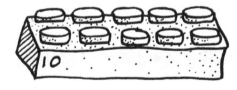 **X3**

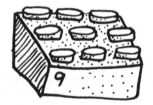 **X3**

 X3

 **X3**

Use three of each kind of block.

What did you build?

_____

248

FiNiSH the PictURe

COMIC BOOK FONT WRITING PRACTICE

Try different comic book writing styles!

DYSLEXIE FONT BY CHRISTIAN BOER:

ABCDEFGHIJKLMNOPQRSTUVWXYZ

abcdefghijklmnopqrstuvwxyz

Create Your Own Font Here:

LISTENING TIME
CLASSICAL MUSIC, HISTORY & LITERATURE

Listen to Story of the World, an audio book

or classical music. Draw and doodle below.

I am listening to: _____

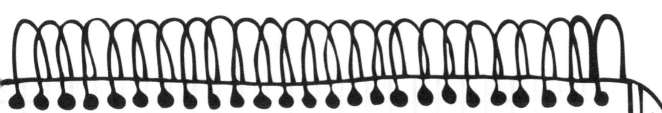

MATH TIME

Use your math book or watch a math tutorial online. Use this graph paper for practice, lessons and notes.

Bonus – Minecraft Math:

You meet a villager. You have 15 emeralds for trading. What can you get?

Answer:_____

_____

_____

MONTH:

January

February

March

April

May

June

July

August

September

October

November

December

Pick an animal to learn about today, draw it:

_____

COLOR ME!

How are you
FEELING TODAY?

DAY:_____

_____

YEAR:_____

ANIMALS OF THE WORLD

What animal are you learning about?

_____

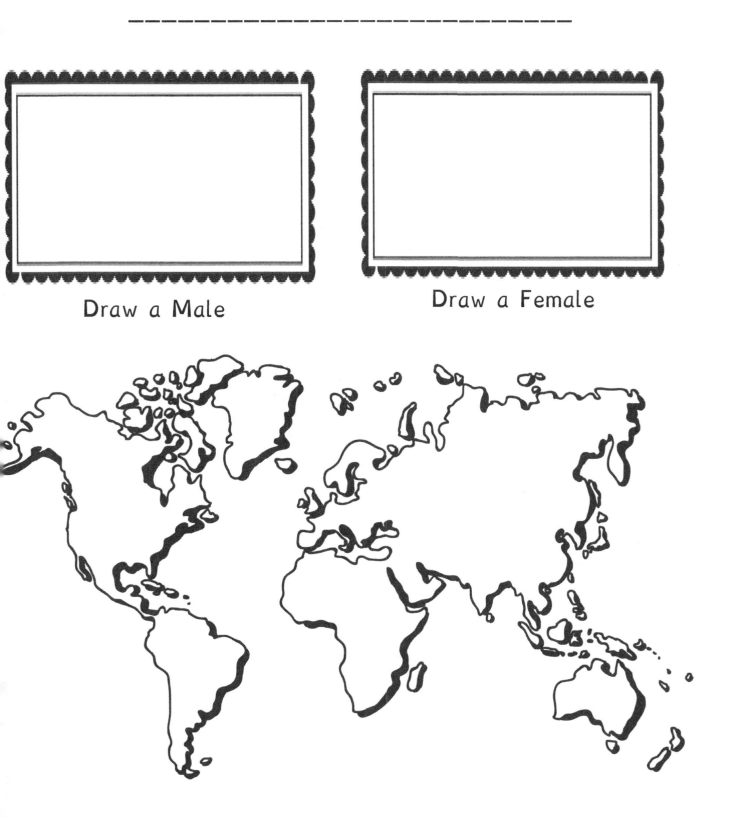

Draw a Male

Draw a Female

Color the parts of the world where this animal lives.

READING TIME

Write and draw about what you are learning.

BACKYARD SCIENCE
NATURE WALK & NATURE STUDY

Draw or write about the things you see outside today.

AN ANIMAL'S LIFE

TYPE OF ANIMAL:_____

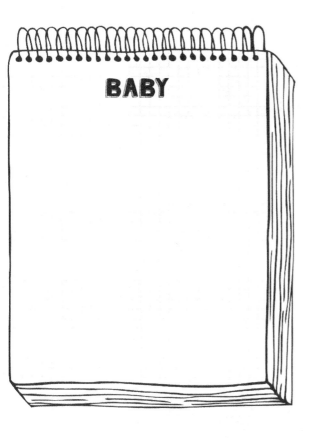

BABY

HABITAT

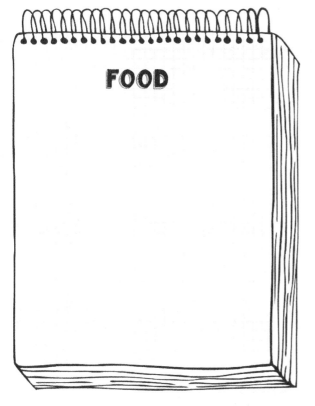

FOOD

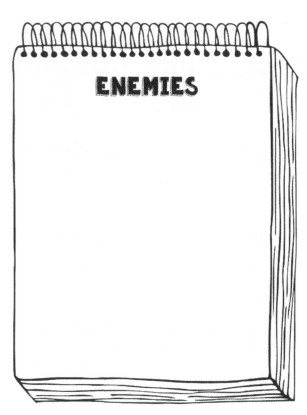

ENEMIES

MOVIE TIME

Watch an Educational Film, Tutorial or Documentary.

TITLE:_____

Draw Your Favorite Scene:

RATING

Write a Review:

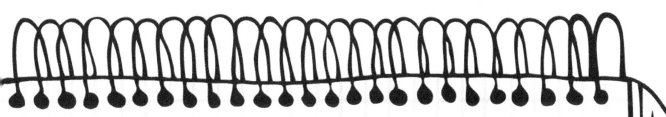

MATH TIME

Use your math book or watch a math tutorial online. Use this graph paper for practice, lessons and notes.

PIXEL ART

Ideas & Inspiration

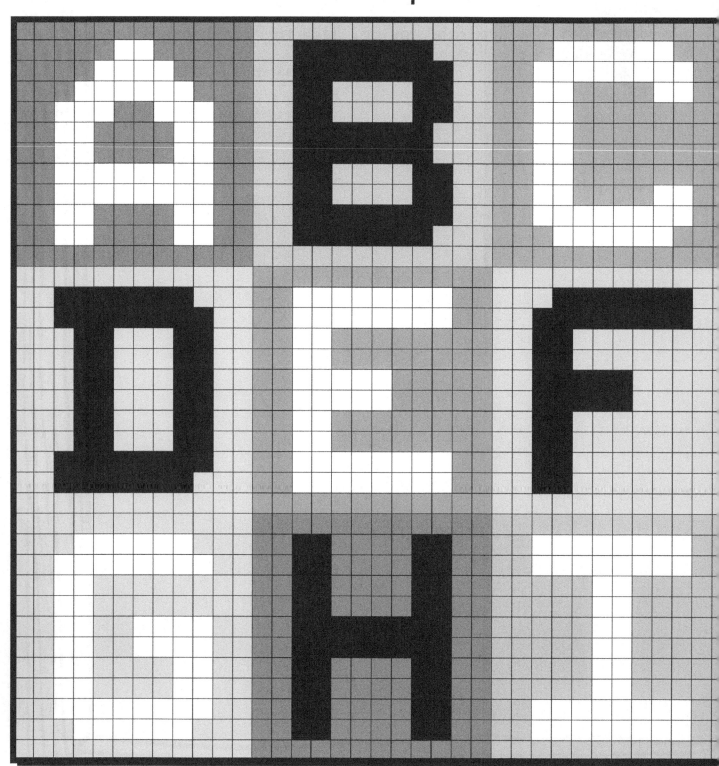

PIXEL ART

Create Your Own Pixel Design

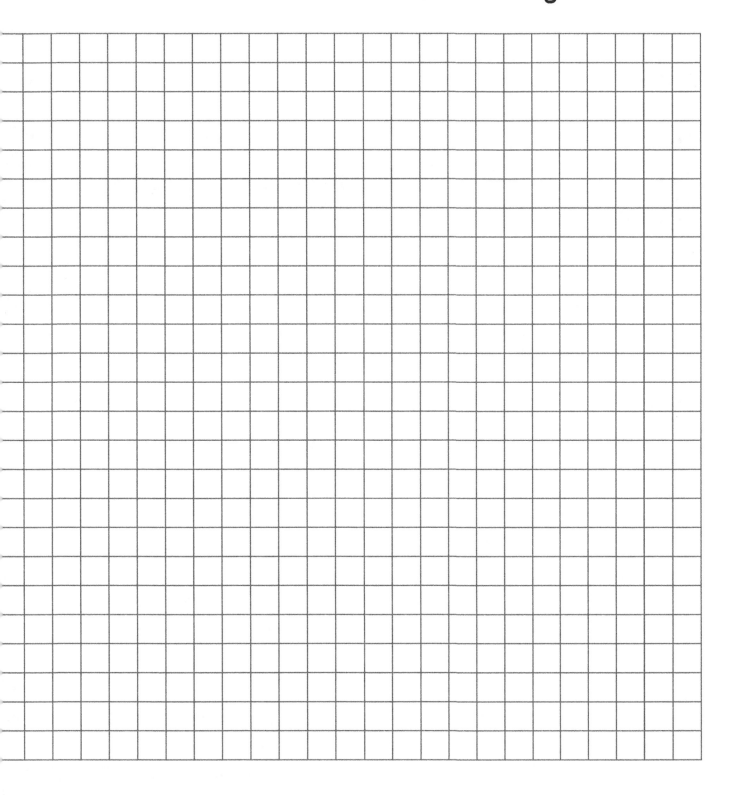

MONTH:

January

February

March

April

May

June

July

August

September

October

November

December

Pick an animal to learn about today, draw it:

_____

COLOR ME!

How are you **FEELING TODAY?**

DAY: _____

_____

YEAR: _____

COPYWORK

Copy a sentence from one of your library books.

TITLE: _____Page#_____

_____

_____

_____

_____

DRAWING TIME

Copy an illustration from one of your books.

READING TIME

Write and draw about
what you are learning.

BACKYARD SCIENCE
NATURE WALK & NATURE STUDY

Draw or write about the things you see outside today.

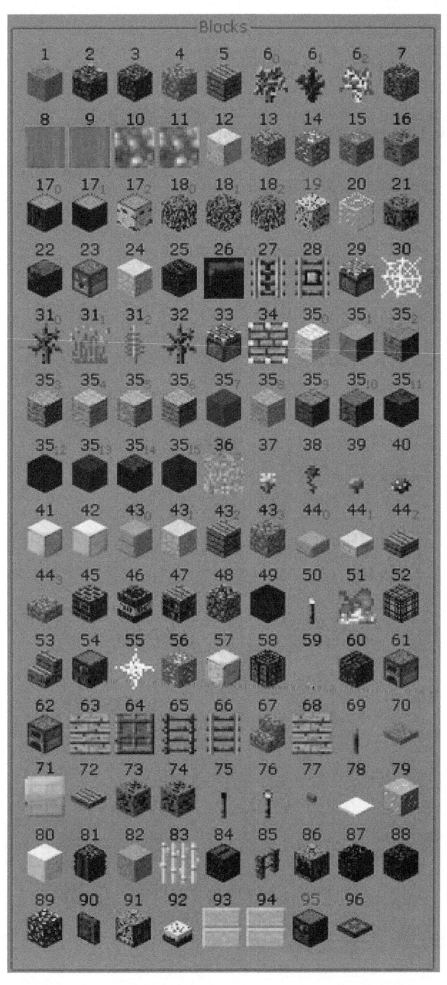

Blocks

MATH PRACTICE

12 x 3	12 x 4
12 x 5	11 x 5
11 x 6	11 x 7
12 x 5	17 x 3
15 x 4	16 x 4

CIRCLE THE ITEMS

That Match Each
Answer

299 + 22	300 + 22
345 + 11	301 + 11
12 + 340	206 + 60
222 + 42	234 + 65
101 + 200	100 + 250

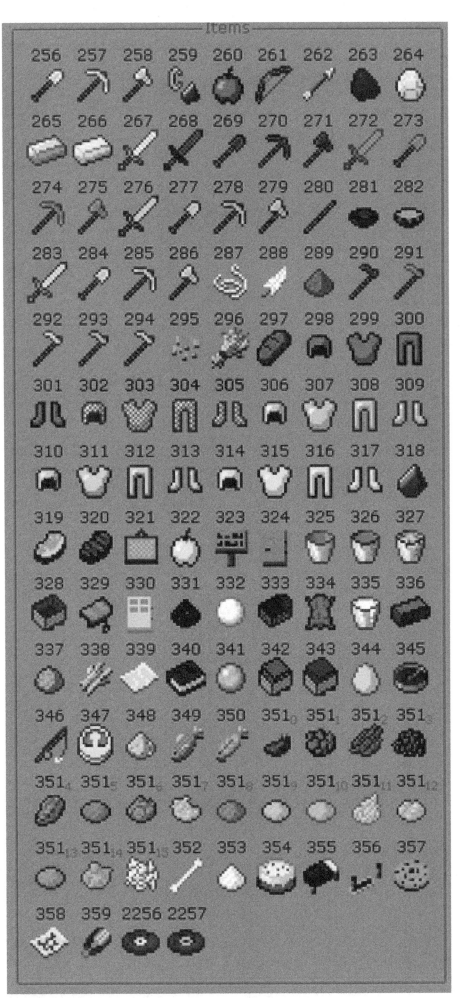

YOU HAVE SEEN THIS ANIMAL ON MINECRAFT.
NOW DESIGN YOUR OWN ANIMAL.

CORE SUBJECTS - LEARNING TIME

Read __ pages in Your Science, Social Studies
& History Books. Write, Draw & Copy Important Information

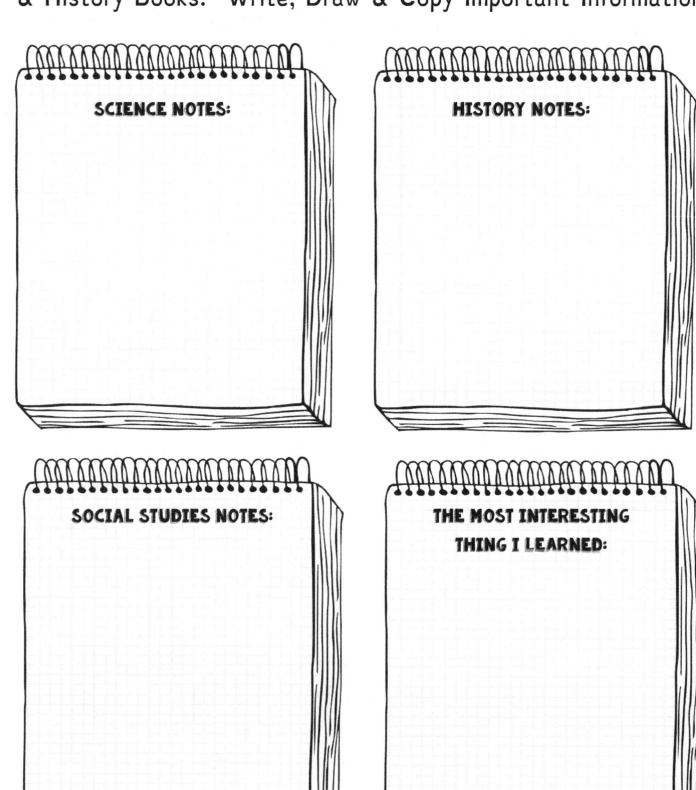

SCIENCE NOTES:

HISTORY NOTES:

SOCIAL STUDIES NOTES:

**THE MOST INTERESTING
THING I LEARNED:**

SPELLING TIME

WORD HUNT

Choose A Letter

____

Find 10 words that include this letter.

1._____

2._____

3._____

4._____

5._____

6._____

7._____

8._____

9._____

10._____

MINECRAFT

Draw and Label Four Elements

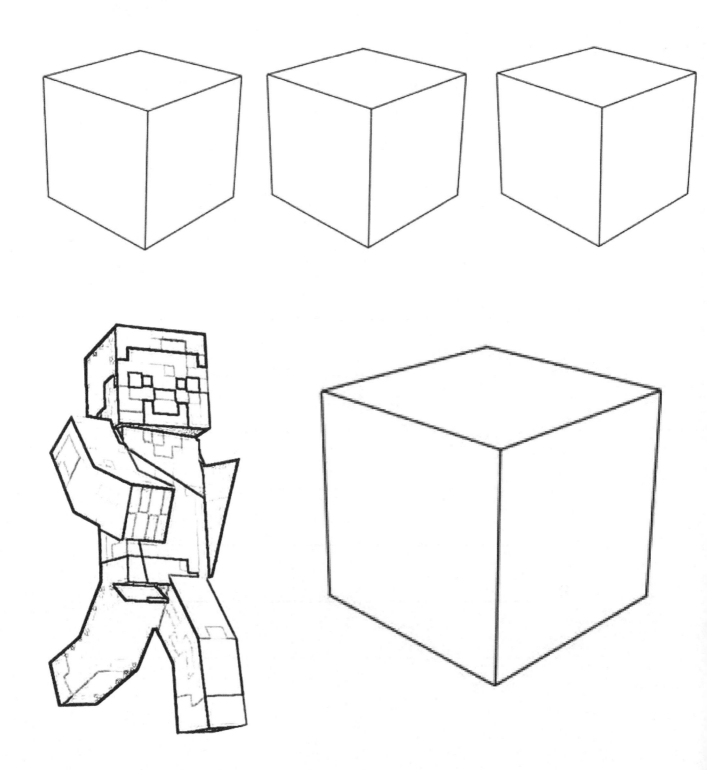

MOVIE TIME

Watch an Educational Film, Tutorial or Documentary.

TITLE:_____

RATING

Draw Your Favorite Scene:

Write a Review:

_____

_____

_____

_____

_____

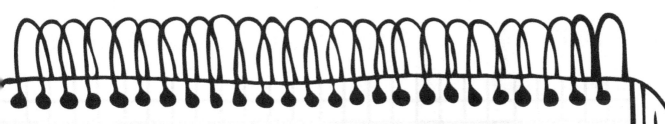

MATH TIME

Use your math book or watch a math
tutorial online. Use this graph paper for
practice, lessons and notes.

MONTH:

January
February
March
April
May
June
July
August
September
October
November
December

Pick an animal to learn about today, draw it:

_____

COLOR ME!

How are you FEELING TODAY?

DAY:_____

_____

YEAR:_____

DRAW A FARM

WHat CaN YOU BuiLd?

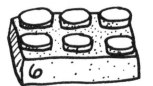 X4

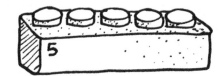 X4

 X4

 X4

 X4

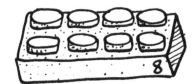 X4

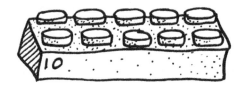 X4

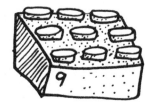 X4

 X4

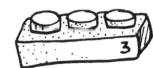 X4

Use four of each kind of block.

What did you build?

_____

FiNiSH the PictURE

READING TIME

Write and draw about
what you are learning.

BACKYARD SCIENCE
NATURE WALK & NATURE STUDY

Draw or write about the things you see outside today.

SPELLING TIME

WORD HUNT

Choose A Letter

_ _ _ _

Find 10 words that include this letter.

1._ _

2._ _

3._ _

4._ _

5._ _

6._ _ _ _ _ _ _ _ _ _ _ _ _ _ _

7._ _ _ _ _ _ _ _ _ _ _ _ _ _ _

8._ _ _ _ _ _ _ _ _ _ _ _ _ _ _

9._ _ _ _ _ _ _ _ _ _ _ _ _ _ _

10._ _ _ _ _ _ _ _ _ _ _ _ _ _

ANIMALS OF THE WORLD

What animal are you learning about?

_____

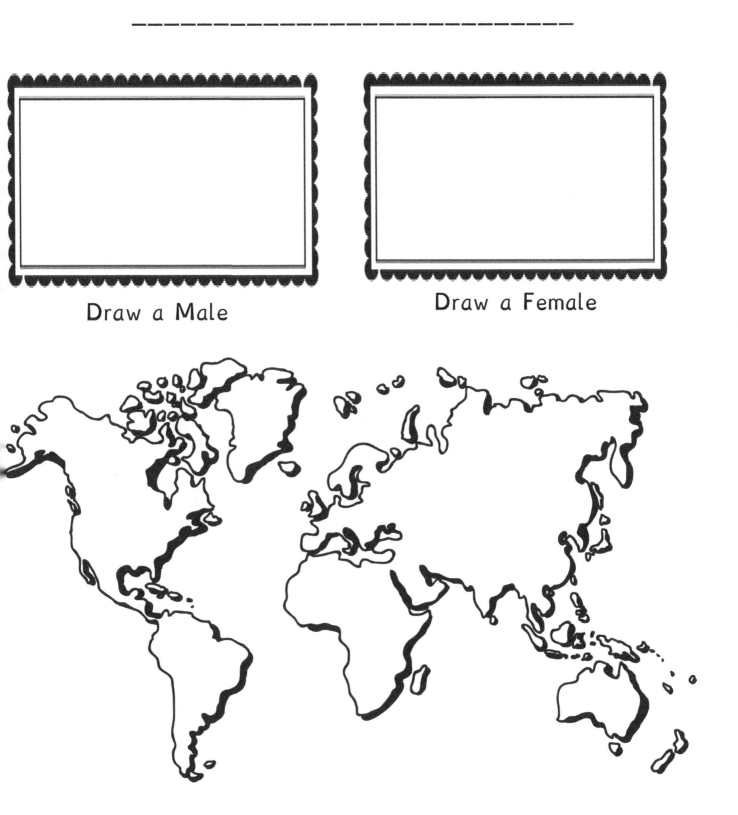

Draw a Male

Draw a Female

Color the parts of the world where this animal lives.

MOVIE TIME

Watch an Educational Film, Tutorial or Documentary.

TITLE:_____

RATING

Draw Your Favorite Scene:

Write a Review:

MATH TIME

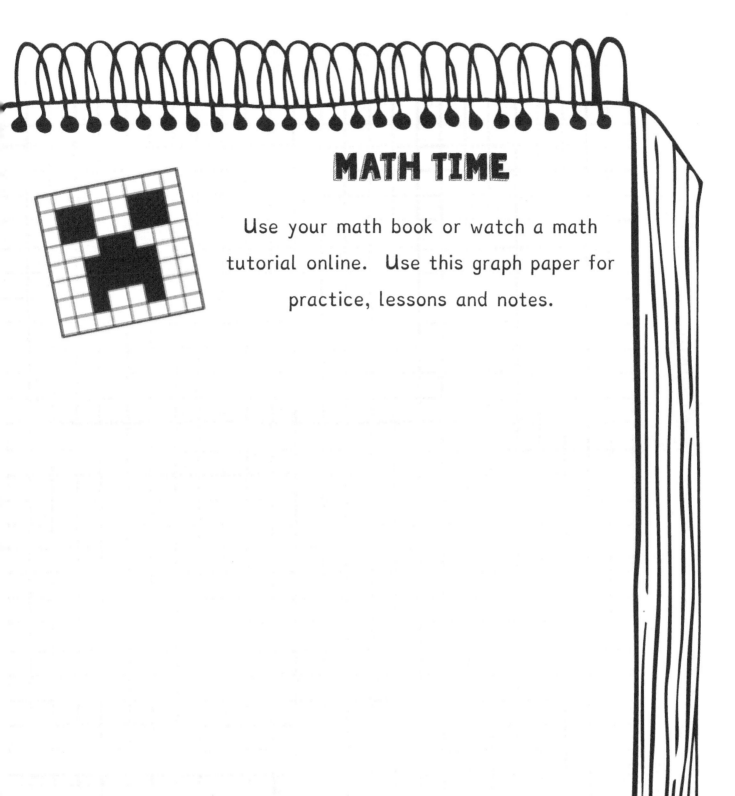

Use your math book or watch a math tutorial online. Use this graph paper for practice, lessons and notes.

MONTH:

January

February

March

April

May

June

July

August

September

October

November

December

Pick an animal to learn about today, draw it:

_____

COLOR ME!

How are you FEELING TODAY?

DAY:_____

YEAR:_____

YOU HAVE SEEN THIS ANIMAL ON MINECRAFT. NOW DESIGN YOUR OWN ANIMAL.

CREATE YOUR OWN CRAFTING RECIPE

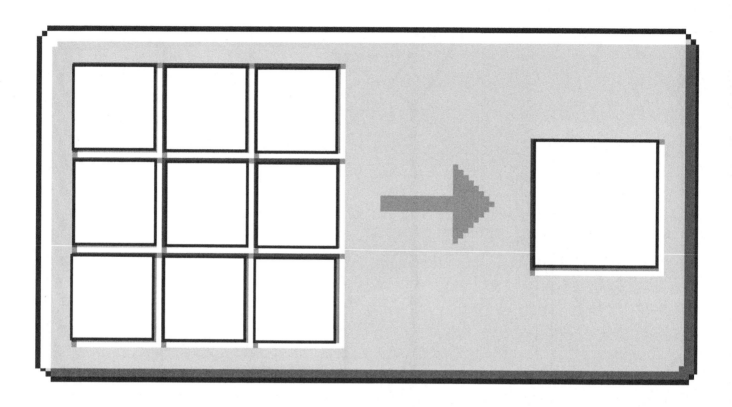

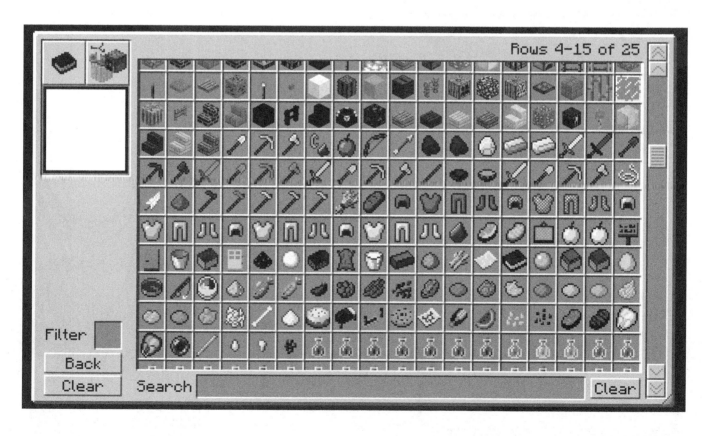

Filter

Back

Clear

Search

Clear

BRAIN GAMES

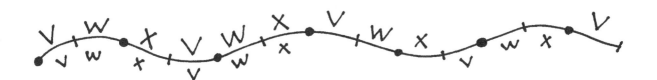

DRAW ANYTHING

MINECRAFT VS. THE REAL WORLD
Discussion and Research Prompts
For Parents and Students

1. Sheering sheep in the real world vs. Minecraft.

2. Difference in beef cows and dairy cows.

3. How to milk a cow in real life vs. Minecraft.

4. Harvesting food in the real world vs Minecraft.

5. How we use cows for food and clothing in the real world vs. Minecraft.

6. Lifecycle of a chicken.

7. Different uses for chickens' real world vs. Minecraft.

8. Protecting your livestock in real life vs. Minecraft.

9. Riding horses in real life vs. the Minecraft world.

10. What is the difference in horses, mules, and donkeys?

11. Why were windmills used on a farm?

12. Milking cows in the past vs. the present.

13. Which tools in Minecraft could be used for real world farming?